# the food of thailand

# the food of thailand

## a journey for food lovers

Photography by Alan Benson
Text by Lulu Grimes
Recipes by Oi Cheepchaiissara

whitecap

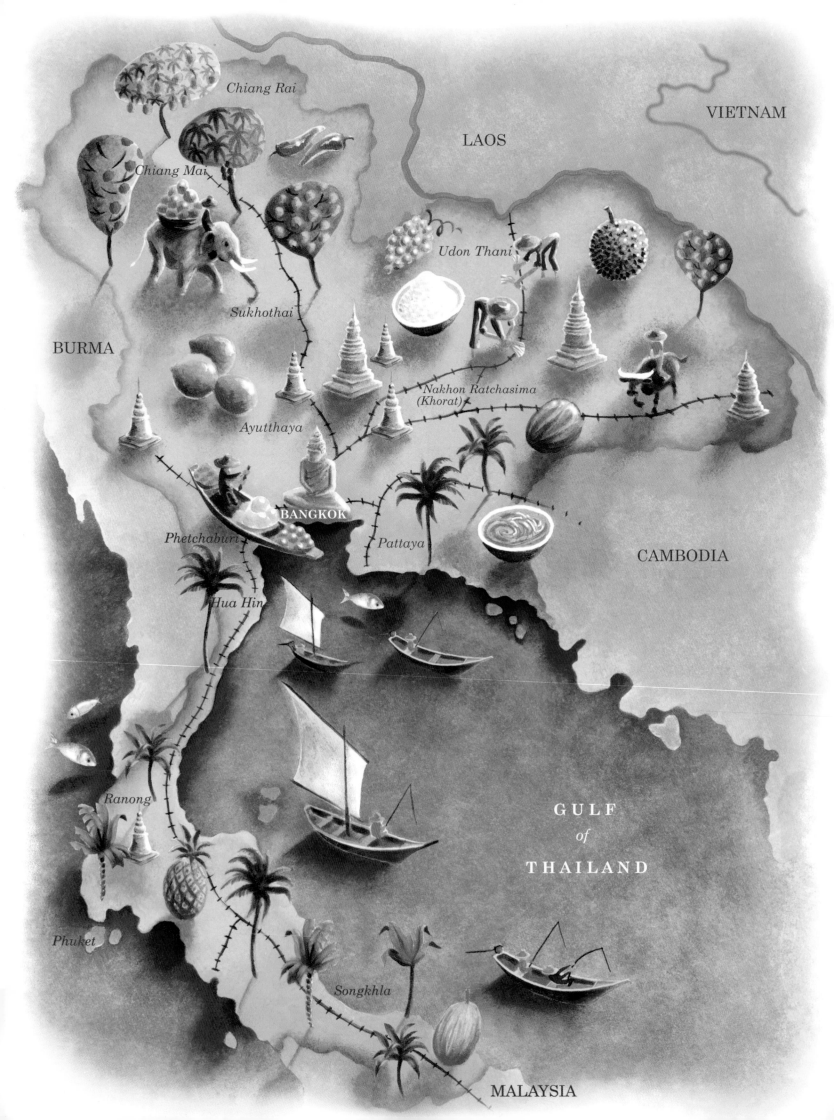

# CONTENTS

## FOOD JOURNEYS IN THAILAND

# the food of
# THAILAND

THAILAND, FOR CENTURIES A STOP-OFF FOR THE TRADERS MOVING BETWEEN SOUTH-EAST ASIA, INDIA, CHINA AND BEYOND, HAS VERY SKILFULLY ASSIMILATED INFLUENCES FROM OTHER COUNTRIES INTO ITS OWN DISTINCTIVE CUISINE WITHOUT COMPROMISING LOCAL CULTURE AND RITUALS.

Despite acting as a trade conduit throughout its history, Thailand, unlike many other Asian nations, has never been ruled by a European power. Mystical and exotic, Siam, as Thailand was once known, managed simultaneously to charm, manipulate and resist her European visitors. Closer neighbours were not so easily rebuffed and Thailand was periodically invaded, most notably by Burma. Despite these incursions, Thailand's remarkably stable religious (Buddhist) and cultural history, coupled with an abundance of locally grown food, is reflected in its historic cuisine. Buddhism permeates all aspects of Thai life. Most men spend at least three months of their young lives as a monk and, as monks are fed by everyone else in the community as a mark of respect, so food and religion are bound together.

The basic tenets of Thai cuisine are ancient in origin and were upheld for centuries by the royal kitchens while being supplemented by many outside influences. Even though they are worlds apart in terms of wealth, the underlying ingredients and recipes used, as well as styles of cooking, were, and still are, not much different between court and country. Presentation, with intricate artistry employed, and, to a certain extent, the superior quality of ingredients available to the court, were what elevated the cuisine of the royal kitchens above that of the common people. Palaces put much effort into teaching culinary skills and crafts in order to maintain their proud reputations.

Rice is central to Thai culture and cuisine. Banana leaves are used as receptacles for snacks sold on the streets. Young monks ride on river boats along the Chaophraya in Bangkok. Bananas are seen growing all over Thailand. Delicious street food is available at night markets. A woman keeps cool in a traditional hat. Ornate architecture on Wat Saen Fang in Chiang Mai.

Dried seafood is a popular ingredient, the fish caught from waters such as these around Phang-nga. Fresh produce such as rambutans and green mango is sold whole, or, like the preserved lotus root, ready to eat. The charming wai greeting is used as a logo. Sugar, chillies with vinegar, chilli sauce and fish sauce are used as seasonings. Herbs are an essential flavouring.

### INFLUENCES

Geographically, culinary ideas have seeped into Thailand through the permeable borders with Malaysia, Laos, Cambodia and Burma. China, who had a far reaching influence on the entire region, has also made her mark on Thai cuisine. As would be expected, influences are strongest nearest the borders. The dishes found along the Mekong River have close affiliations to Laos, Cambodia and Vietnam. Around Chiang Mai there are Burmese-style curries and soups, and close to Malaysia, Muslim recipes such as massaman and roti are common.

The most significant addition to Thai cuisine came not from Asia but from South America, via Europe. In the sixteenth century the Portuguese introduced what was to become one of the hallmarks of the cuisine, the chilli. Thai cuisine, like that of other cultures which accepted the chilli so readily, had long included an element of heat by way of fresh green peppercorns, dried white peppercorns and galangal. As well, foreign *(farang)* vegetables and fruit have been cultivated for the last couple of centuries: tomatoes, eggplants (aubergines), asparagus, carrots (known as orange long turnips), snow peas (mangetout) and corn are common.

### EATING THAI FOOD

With the exception of snacks such as noodles, green papaya salad, or a single portion of curry over rice, Thai food is, on the whole, made to be shared. Portions are served on platters and meant for at least two people. Everything on the table is an accompaniment to rice, the most important component of the meal. Generally the rice is served with a curry, a fish dish, a stir-fry, a salad, a soup and vegetables. All the food is served at once. Unlike European tradition, soups come in a large bowl and are eaten with the meal, not before it. Meals begin when the host says *kin khao* or 'eat rice'. The food is not necessarily eaten piping hot.

### ETIQUETTE

Thai people eat with a spoon and fork, the fork being used to push food onto the spoon or to pick up pieces of meat or sliced fruit. Chopsticks are only used with noodles, and sticky rice and its accompaniments are eaten using the right hand. When eating in Thailand there are further subtle areas of etiquette to be observed. Platters of food are left on the table, and not passed around, as stretching is not considered rude and someone on the other side of the table will always be happy to spoon things onto your plate. You should only take a couple of spoonfuls of each dish at a time as an accompaniment to rice.

## THE FOOD OF THE NORTH-EAST

This region is known as Isaan and the food of the region is identified by the same name. Most of the area is a high plateau divided by the Phu Phan mountains. Divided from the rest of Thailand by more mountains, Laos and Cambodia, just over the border, have had a strong culinary influence, with much of the cuisines overlapping. The Mekong River flows along the border with both countries and has been the main means of trade for centuries.

North-Eastern Thailand was one of the first areas in Asia to grow rice. Rice is cultivated over much of the plateau but, unlike in other areas of Thailand, rain is less reliable, thus making the yield patchy. Sticky rice is preferred in the countryside and long-grain rice in the cities. As much of the area is poorer than the rest of the country, food reflects this. Rice is a staple and dishes that are served with it are small in quantity but very pungent in flavour. Unfermented fish sauce and chillies are the main seasonings. Commonly used pickled and preserved foods are another symptom of an unreliable food supply and also add more flavour to a diet of rice in this form than their original fresh state.

*Kai yang* or *kai ping*, grilled chicken, is found all over the area, often sold by roadside vendors. The chicken skin is rubbed with garlic, fish sauce, coriander (cilantro) root or lemon grass and black pepper, then the chicken is usually flattened and pinned on a bamboo skewer before being barbecued over coals and served with a chilli dipping sauce. Chicken is also made into *laap*, a minced meat salad made with lime juice, fish sauce, lemon grass, chillies or chilli powder and *khao khua pon*, roasted rice. Duck, fish and buffalo are also used to make *laap,* and *neu naam tok*, grilled strips of beef, are used for similar salads.

*Som tam*, a green papaya salad with chillies, peanuts, cherry tomatoes and dried shrimp, is a popular snack. Individual portions are pounded together by hand and eaten with sticky rice. The addition of pickled crabs transforms *som tam* into a Laotian-style dish. Soups are hot and sour style *tom*, or spicy style, *sukii*. *Sukii* are served in steamboats and each person dips in and cooks their own set of ingredients. The very south of the region has some coconut milk in soups.

Insects and frogs are popular, and red ants are used as a souring agent in some dishes. Fish are freshwater, the Mekong River being famous for the giant catfish caught from it, mainly in the months of April and May.

Roast chicken is a popular street food. Cooked frogs and insects are eaten in the North. The sun sets over the Mekong River with Thailand in the distance. Rickshaws are a popular form of transport in Udon Thani. Common street snacks include freshly prepared bamboo shoot salad and green papaya salad, as well as sticky rice, often served on banana leaves.

Stalls and markets are prevalent in Thailand: roasted vegetables are beautifully laid out on a vegetable stall, cut fresh fruit is sold in plastic bags, and prepared *naam phrik* can be bought at Warorot market in Chiang Mai. Workers in the paddy fields near Chiang Rai. A typical Akha tribal headdress. Corn is grown in the hills near Mae Salong in the northern regions.

## THE FOOD OF THE NORTH

Northern Thailand, which is the area bordered by Burma to the west and Laos to the east, has always had a strong regional identity that is distinctively different from the Thailand of the South and of the Centre. Hill tribes farm the hillsides, growing corn and rice, and families work as collectives, helping each other during the planting and harvest time. The cooler climate of the hills means that many types of European fruit grow well there, so peaches, apples and strawberries are found growing alongside lychees. Non-indigenous vegetables such as asparagus, snow peas (mangetout) and corn are also cultivated.

Above all the other dishes of the area, Northern Thai curries have Burmese influences. Made without coconut milk, they are fiery and thinner in consistency. *Kaeng hangleh muu*, Chiang Mai pork curry, is the most famous. *Naam phrik*, chilli dips, are also popular, served with cooked or raw vegetables and crunchy pieces of deep-fried pork rind.

Pork is more popular in this region, eaten both in its natural state and made into sausages. *Naem maw*, fermented sausages made with pork rind and sticky rice, are common, as are *sai ua*, bright red sausages made with pork and chillies. German-style frankfurters appear in salads and this is just one of the influences that American soldiers, stationed in the area during the Vietnam war, had on the cuisine.

*Khao niaw*, sticky rice, is the preferred rice, eaten with dishes such as *naam phrik*, *som tam* or pomelo salad and with *kaeng hangleh muu*. Many dishes are always served with sticky rice. Sticky rice can be bought ready-cooked wrapped in banana leaves, or in plastic bags, at markets.

Noodles are popular due to the large amounts of Chinese (Shan and Yunnanese) and Burmese people who live in the area. *Khao sawy*, flat egg noodles with curry, is a speciality of Chiang Mai, sold by Yunnanese noodle vendors near the mosques. *Khanom jiin* and *kuaytiaw* (types of rice noodles) are also popular and *wun sen*, mung bean noodles, are used in salads and soups as well as being wrapped in rice paper rolls in the same way as Vietnamese spring rolls.

Formal meals are served in small bowls on a *khao niaw*, teak platter. This is a revival of old-style serving that has become popular once again. Another speciality of the area is insects. Deep-fried bamboo worm, water beetles and various other insects are sold as snacks.

## THE FOOD OF THE CENTRE AND BANGKOK

Central Thailand runs upwards from the Isthmus of Kra and encompasses the plains north of Bangkok. To the East it stretches to the Cambodian border, and to the West as far as Burma. Much of this area, which is watered by many rivers, constitutes the rice-bowl of Thailand. A network of canals further irrigates the region, as well as providing a means of transport. Paddy fields cover most of the area, but fruit, sugar cane, maize, peanuts and taro are also cultivated on a large scale.

Though most of this area has no access to the sea, the waterways provide a host of freshwater fish, prawns (shrimp) and crabs. Crabs and fish even live amongst the paddy as do the frogs and water beetles that are commonly eaten. Chicken, pork and beef feature in the cuisine, alongside the fish. The fertility of these regions means many vegetables grow easily and cultivated vegetables include the popular Thai eggplants (aubergines), *cha-om* (a bitter green vegetable that resembles a fern), and bamboo shoots, as well as snake beans and European vegetables like tomatoes. Vegetables grown in or alongside the waterways include *phak bung* (water spinach) and lotus shoots.

The cuisine of the Centre is what is generally considered to be 'classic Thai' and includes what are probably the most recognizable Thai dishes. Curries include red, green and *phanaeng* (panaeng). Soups are *tom khaa kai*, *tom yam* and *kaeng jeut* (bland soup); *yam* (salads) are popular as are stir-fries. Dishes influenced by the Chinese include those baked in clay pots, various noodle dishes as well as some braised dishes flavoured with Chinese spices. Japanese-style *sukii* (similar to sukiyaki) is also available.

Seasonings are classic, designed to give the typical hot, sour, salty and sweet combination. The use of palm sugar makes many recipes sweeter than their southern counterparts. Si Racha on the Gulf of Thailand is famous for the chilli sauce made there and it appears as a condiment on virtually every table.

Bangkok, or Krung Thep, to use the abbreviated Thai name, is the modern home of royal Thai cuisine. In 1960, King Bhumibol allowed the court cookbooks to be opened to everyone and dishes such as roast duck curry became accessible. Restaurants specialize in these dishes and are the best place to sample such delights.

Fresh rice noodles are sold at Aw Taw Kaw market in Bangkok. An endearing girl looks curiously at the camera in Bangkok. A giant gold Buddha dominates the scene on the road to Khorat. Vegetables on sale at Aw Taw Kaw market. Frantic Bangkok, Thailand's capital, contrasts with the serenity of transport boats used around the quiet khlongs of Damnoen Saduak.

Lunch at a beachside cafe
includes fresh local fish.
Palm trees line roads and
waterways. Fishermen in
longtail boats fish near
Phang-nga. Coconuts
are ubiquitous in the South:
seen growing, being cracked
for meat, and young
coconuts being sold for their
liquid. Lemon grass is one
of the main flavours in Thai
cooking. Fish is displayed
at Ranong fish market.

## THE FOOD OF THE SOUTH

The fourteen provinces that make up the area between the Isthmus of Kra (the narrowest point in Thailand) and the Malaysian border have always been culturally different from the rest of the country. Once under the influence of the ancient Indonesian Sriwijaya empire along with areas of Malaysia, Malay-Indonesian culture and religion is still apparent in the life and language of the South.

The provinces closest to Malaysia have large numbers of Muslims, mostly concentrated around the coast and on surrounding islands where they make their living by fishing. Buddhist Thai people farm the inland regions and a Chinese minority mainly live and work in the cities.

Seafood and fish are the predominate feature of southern cuisine and are acceptable to all, both culturally and in regard to religion. With the advantage of two long coastlines, fresh fish and seafood is eaten in abundance. It is grilled over charcoal, used in stir-fries or curries, and even more of it is preserved by drying. Racks of dried squid and cottonfish line many coastal roads. Locally made shrimp paste and fish sauce are used in quantity.

The South is also the land of the palm tree. Coconut and oil palms are 'farmed' in plantations as well as growing wild, fringing the beaches on both coasts. Further up the Isthmus, sugar palms are grown for their sweet sap. Phuket is home to many pineapple plantations and rice is cultivated wherever it can be persuaded to grow.

There are three main styles of cooking. Thai (Buddhist) curries and soups are often tempered and enriched by the addition of coconut milk or cream. Spices include turmeric and pepper, and chillies are used with abandon. 'Yellow' curries are popular. Muslim dishes use ghee and oil rather than coconut and use a larger range of fragrant spices including cardamom, cumin and cloves. *Kaeng matsaman*, an Indian-style curry, is at its best in the South. Indo-Malay dishes such as satay are popular as are Indian-style roti. Chinese-style dishes include *khanom jiin* (Chinese-style rice noodles), barbecued meats, various deep-fried snacks, steamed buns, and dumplings.

Coffee shops sell *kopi* (filtered coffee), and this, served with *khao yam* (cooked dry rice, toasted coconut, makrut (kaffir) lime leaves, bean sprouts and lemon grass), makes a typical breakfast in the southern areas of Thailand.

SNACKS &
STREET FOOD

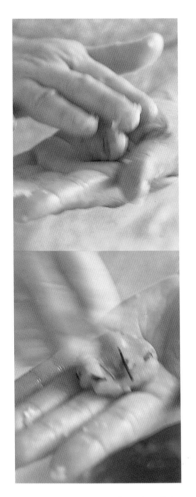

THAWT MAN PLAA

# FRIED FISH CAKES WITH GREEN BEANS

FISH CAKES ARE JUST ONE OF MANY DELICIOUS SNACKS SOLD AS STREET FOOD IN THAILAND. BATCHES ARE FRIED ON REQUEST AND SERVED IN A PLASTIC BAG, ALONG WITH A BAMBOO SKEWER FOR EATING THEM AND A SMALL BAG OF SAUCE FOR ADDITIONAL FLAVOUR.

450 g (1 lb) firm white fish fillets
1 tablespoon red curry paste
   (page 276) or bought paste
1 tablespoon fish sauce
1 egg
50 g (2 oz) snake beans,
   finely sliced
5 makrut (kaffir) lime leaves,
   finely shredded
peanut oil, for deep-frying
sweet chilli sauce (page 284),
   to serve
cucumber relish (page 287),
   to serve

MAKES 30

REMOVE any skin and bone from the fish and roughly chop the flesh. In a food processor or a blender, mince the fish fillets until smooth. Add the curry paste, fish sauce and egg, then blend briefly until smooth. Spoon into a bowl and mix in the beans and makrut lime leaves. Use wet hands to shape the fish paste into thin, flat cakes, about 5 cm (2 inches) across, using about a tablespoon of mixture for each.

HEAT 5 cm (2 inches) oil in a wok or deep frying pan over a medium heat. When the oil seems hot, drop a small piece of fish cake into it. If it sizzles immediately, the oil is ready.

LOWER five or six of the fish cakes into the oil and deep-fry them until they are golden brown on both sides and very puffy. Remove with a slotted spoon and drain on paper towels. Keep the cooked fish cakes warm while deep-frying the rest. Serve hot with sweet chilli sauce and cucumber relish.

FOR a variation make up another batch of the fish mixture but leave out the curry paste. Cook as above and serve both types together.

Using wet hands makes the fish mixture less likely to stick to your hands and also easier to handle.

SOM TAM MALAKAW

# GREEN PAPAYA SALAD

THIS DISH FROM THE NORTH-EAST IS NOW POPULAR THROUGHOUT THAILAND. SOM MEANS 'SOUR', AND TUM MEANS 'POUND' (WITH A PESTLE AND MORTAR). MULTIPLY THE INGREDIENTS BY THE NUMBER OF PORTIONS BUT MAKE JUST ONE SERVE AT A TIME OTHERWISE IT WON'T FIT IN YOUR MORTAR.

120 g (4 oz) small hard, green, unripe papaya
1½ tablespoons palm sugar
1 tablespoon fish sauce
1–2 garlic cloves
25 g (1 oz) roasted peanuts
25 g (1 oz) snake beans cut into 2.5 cm (1 inch) pieces
1 tablespoon ground dried shrimp
2–6 bird's eye chillies, stems removed (6 will give a very hot result)
50 g (2 oz) cherry tomatoes, left whole, or 2 medium tomatoes, cut into 6 wedges
half a lime
sticky rice (page 280), to serve

SERVES 1

PEEL the green papaya with a vegetable peeler and cut the papaya into long, thin shreds. If you have a mandolin, use the grater attachment.

MIX the palm sugar with the fish sauce until the sugar has dissolved.

USING a large, deep pestle and mortar, pound the garlic into a paste. Add the roasted peanuts and pound roughly together with the garlic. Add the papaya and pound softly, using a spoon to scrape down the sides, and turning and mixing well.

ADD the beans, dried shrimp and chillies and keep pounding and turning to bruise these ingredients. Add the sugar mixture and tomatoes, squeeze in the lime juice and add the lime skin to the mixture. Lightly pound together for another minute until thoroughly mixed. As the juice comes out, pound more gently so the liquid doesn't splash. Discard the lime skin. Taste the sauce in the bottom of the mortar and adjust the seasoning if necessary. It should be a balance of sweet and sour with a hot and salty taste.

SPOON the papaya salad and all the juices onto a serving plate. Serve with sticky rice.

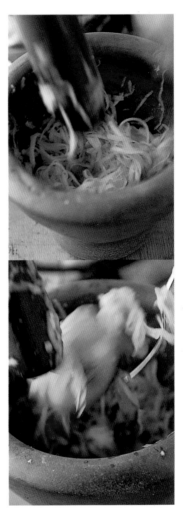

Only one portion of the salad at a time will fit into your mortar.

Cooking satay at Aw Taw Kaw market in Bangkok.

Mixing the marinade into the chicken with your fingers will help ensure all the pieces are coated.

SA-TE KAI

# CHICKEN SATAY

ORIGINATING IN INDONESIA, SATAY HAS MADE ITS WAY NORTH AND HAS BEEN ADAPTED TO SUIT LOCAL TASTE. SATAY SHOULD BE COOKED QUICKLY OVER HOT CHARCOALS. TRADITIONALLY SERVED WITH PEANUT SAUCE, IT IS ALSO DELICIOUS WITH CUCUMBER RELISH OR SWEET CHILLI SAUCE.

1 kg (2 lb 4 oz) skinless chicken breast fillets

MARINADE
2–3 Asian shallots, roughly chopped
4–5 garlic cloves, roughly chopped
4 coriander (cilantro) roots, finely chopped
2.5 cm (1 inch) piece of ginger, sliced
1 tablespoon roasted ground coriander
1 tablespoon roasted ground cumin
1 tablespoon roasted ground turmeric
1 teaspoon Thai curry powder (page 287) or bought Thai curry powder
2 tablespoons light soy sauce
4 tablespoons vegetable oil
410 ml (1⅔ cups) coconut milk (page 279)
2 tablespoons palm sugar
1½ teaspoons salt
40 bamboo sticks, about 18–20 cm (7–8 inches) long
peanut sauce (page 284) or cucumber relish (page 287), to serve

MAKES 40 STICKS

CUT the chicken fillets into strips 4 cm (1½ inches) wide x 10 cm (4 inches) long x 5 mm (¼ inch) thick and put them in a bowl.

USING a food processor, blender or pestle and mortar, blend or pound the shallots, garlic, coriander roots and ginger to a paste.

ADD the paste to the chicken, along with the ground coriander, cumin, turmeric, curry powder, light soy sauce, vegetable oil, coconut milk, sugar and salt. Mix with your fingers or a spoon until the chicken is well coated. Cover with plastic wrap and marinate in the refrigerator for at least 5 hours, or overnight. Turn the chicken occasionally.

SOAK the bamboo sticks in water for 1 hour to prevent them from burning during cooking.

THREAD a piece of the marinated chicken onto each stick as if you were sewing a piece of material. If the pieces are small, thread two pieces onto each stick.

HEAT a barbecue or grill (broiler) to high. If using the grill, line the tray with foil.

BARBECUE the satay sticks for 5 to 7 minutes on each side, or grill (broil) for 10 minutes on each side, until the chicken is cooked through and slightly charred. Turn frequently and brush the marinade sauce over the meat during cooking. If using the grill, cook a good distance below the heat. Serve hot with peanut sauce or cucumber relish.

KHAO NIAW NA KUNG

# STICKY RICE WITH SHRIMP OR COCONUT TOPPING

SHRIMP TOPPING
2 garlic cloves, roughly chopped
4 coriander (cilantro) roots, cleaned
¼ teaspoon ground black pepper
1 tablespoon vegetable oil
200 g (7 oz) minced (ground) shrimp
    or very small raw prawns (shrimp)
25 g (1 oz) grated coconut
1 teaspoon fish sauce
3 tablespoons sugar

OR

COCONUT TOPPING
150 g (5 oz) grated coconut or
    desiccated coconut
150 g (5 oz) palm sugar

1 quantity of sticky rice with
    coconut milk (page 280)
3 makrut (kaffir) lime leaves,
    finely sliced, for garnish

SERVES 4

TO MAKE the shrimp topping, use a pestle and mortar to pound the garlic, coriander roots and pepper to a smooth paste. Alternatively, chop with a sharp knife until smooth. Heat the oil in a wok or frying pan and stir-fry the garlic mixture over a medium heat until fragrant. Add the minced shrimp or prawns, coconut, fish sauce and sugar and stir-fry for 3 to 4 minutes or until the minced shrimp is cooked. Taste, then adjust the seasoning if necessary. The flavour should be sweet and lightly salty.

TO MAKE the coconut topping, mix the coconut, sugar, 125 ml (½ cup) water and a pinch of salt in a saucepan and stir over a low heat until the sugar is dissolved. Do not let it thicken to a point where it will harden. Remove from the heat.

SERVE by filling a small, wet bowl with the sticky rice and turning it out on a small dessert plate. Top with shrimp or coconut topping and a sprinkle of lime leaves. You can use half of each topping if you like.

STEAMED EGGS

KAI TUN

# STEAMED EGGS

2 large eggs
2 teaspoons light soy sauce
1 spring onion (scallion), finely sliced
a pinch of ground white pepper
1½ tablespoons vegetable oil
3–4 garlic cloves, finely chopped
a few coriander (cilantro) leaves,
    for garnish
1–2 long red chillies, thinly sliced,
    for garnish

SERVES 2

BEAT the eggs in a bowl with a fork. Mix in 170 ml (⅔ cup) water and the soy sauce, spring onion and pepper. Divide between two small heatproof bowls.

FILL a wok or steamer pan with water, cover, bring to a boil, then reduce the heat to medium. Taking care not to burn your hands, place the bowls on the rack of a bamboo steaming basket or on a steamer rack in the wok or pan. Cover the steamer and leave over the simmering water for 13 to 15 minutes or until the eggs set. Test with a skewer or fork. If it comes out clean the eggs are cooked.

HEAT the oil and stir-fry the garlic until golden. Serve the eggs hot or warm, sprinkled with the garlic. Garnish with coriander leaves and chillies.

Put a small amount of filling in the centre of the won ton sheet and gently gather up into a dainty little purse.

# GOLD PURSES

THESE DEEP-FRIED SNACKS ARE AN EXAMPLE OF THE INFLUENCE CHINESE CUISINE HAS HAD IN THAILAND. GOLD PURSES ARE GOOD TO SERVE WITH DRINKS BUT ARE ALSO A NICE WAY TO START A MEAL. THEY CAN BE SERVED WITH A SWEET OR A HOT CHILLI SAUCE, OR SOY SAUCE.

110 g (4 oz) minced (ground) raw
    prawns (shrimp)
80 g (½ cup) water chestnuts,
    drained and roughly chopped
1 garlic clove, finely chopped
1 spring onion (scallion),
    finely chopped
1 tablespoon oyster sauce
¼ teaspoon salt
¼ teaspoon pepper
30–35 won ton sheets 7.5 cm
    (3 inches) square
peanut oil, for deep-frying
sweet chilli sauce (page 284),
    or other chilli sauce, to serve

MAKES ABOUT 30

COMBINE the prawns with the water chestnuts, garlic and spring onion in a bowl. Mix in the oyster sauce, salt and pepper. Spoon about ½ teaspoon of mixture into the middle of each won ton sheet. Gather up, squeezing the corners together to make a little purse. Place on a tray. Continue until you have used up all the sheets and filling.

HEAT 5 cm (2 inches) oil in a wok or deep frying pan over a medium heat. When the oil seems hot, drop a small piece of won ton sheet into the oil. If it sizzles immediately, the oil is ready. Don't have the oil too hot or the purses will burn.

LOWER five purses into the oil. After 2 to 3 minutes they will start to go hard. Lower another four to five purses into the oil and deep-fry them all together. To help cook the tops, spoon some of the oil over the tops. Deep-fry for another 3 to 4 minutes or until golden brown and crispy. As each batch cooks, lift out the purses with a slotted spoon and add some more in their place. Drain on paper towels. Keep warm while deep-frying the remaining purses. Transfer to a serving plate. Serve with chilli sauce.

KARII BUFF
# CURRY PUFFS

### FILLING
1½ tablespoons vegetable oil
2–3 garlic cloves, finely chopped
1 small onion, finely chopped
5 coriander (cilantro) roots,
    finely chopped
200 g (7 oz) minced (ground)
    chicken, pork or raw prawns
    (shrimp)
1 small red capsicum (pepper),
    finely diced
50 g (⅓ cup) peas
350 g (12 oz) potatoes, peeled,
    cooked and cut into small dice
3 tablespoons fish sauce
2 tablespoons sugar
1 teaspoon Thai curry powder
    (page 287) or bought Thai
    curry powder
peanut oil, for deep-frying

### PASTRY A
340 g (2¾ cups) self-raising flour
2 teaspoons sugar
½ teaspoon salt
80 ml (⅓ cup) vegetable oil

### PASTRY B
185 g (1½ cups) self-raising flour
80–125 ml (⅓–½ cup) vegetable oil

MAKES 30

HEAT the oil in a wok or frying pan and stir-fry the garlic. Add the onion and coriander roots and cook over a medium heat for 2 to 3 minutes. Stir in the chicken, breaking it up until it is separated and cooked. Add the capsicum and peas and stir for 1 to 2 minutes. Stir in the potatoes, fish sauce, sugar and curry powder. Adjust the seasoning.

TO MAKE pastry A, combine the flour, sugar and salt in a bowl. Make a well and add the oil. Gradually mix in 125–170 ml (½–⅔ cup) water and gently knead until the dough is smooth. Make 15 balls, place them on a tray and cover with plastic wrap. To make pastry B, lightly mix the flour and oil until the dough just holds together. Make 15 balls, place on a tray and cover.

ROLL a ball of pastry A into a disc, wrap it around a ball of pastry B, then squeeze together. Roll out a 5 x 15 cm (2 x 6 inch) rectangle. Take the short edge and roll it up tightly into a tube. Using a rolling pin, flatten the pastry lengthways to form a rectangle. Repeat one more time, rolling and flattening the pastry. Roll into a tube and cut in half. You should see the different layers of pastry in the cross section. To use, take one half, turn it vertically so it rests on the cut section and roll it into a round sheet. Place a sheet on the work surface and spoon 1–1½ tablespoons of filling onto the middle. Brush the pastry edge with water and fold over to form a semicircle. Press the edges to seal. Make repeated folds on the rounded edge by folding a little piece of the pastry over as you move around the edge. Place on a tray and repeat with the remaining pastry and filling.

HEAT 7.5 cm (3 inches) oil in a wok or deep frying pan over a medium heat. Drop a small piece of pastry into the oil. If it sizzles immediately, the oil is ready. Don't have the oil too hot. Lower in three or four puffs. After 2 minutes they will rise. Lower in another two to three and deep-fry them all together. To help cook the tops, splash oil over the tops. Deep-fry for 3 to 4 minutes until they puff up. As each batch cooks, lift out with a slotted spoon and add more puffs to the oil. Drain on paper towels. Serve hot, warm or cold.

The pastry for these morsels takes a little while to make but the end result is an absolutely delicious crunchy curry puff.

Traditionally, Thais use spring onion greens for tying these bags but you may find it easier to use chives.

THUNG TONG

# GOLD BAGS

THIS DELICATE CHINESE-STYLE STARTER OR SNACK LOOKS EXACTLY AS IT IS DESCRIBED — A TINY GOLD BAG. BLANCHED CHIVES WILL ALSO WORK AS TIES FOR THE TOPS OF THE BAGS. IF YOU LIKE YOU CAN USE HALF PRAWNS AND HALF CHICKEN OR PORK FOR THE FILLING.

280 g (10 oz) raw prawns (shrimp), peeled, deveined and roughly chopped, or skinless chicken or pork fillet, roughly chopped
225 g (8 oz) tin water chestnuts, drained and roughly chopped
3–4 garlic cloves, finely chopped
3 spring onions (scallions), finely sliced
1 tablespoon oyster sauce
1 teaspoon ground white pepper
1 teaspoon salt
2–3 bunches of spring onions (scallions), or 40 chives, for ties
2 tablespoons plain (all-purpose) flour
40 spring roll sheets 13 cm (5 inches) square
peanut oil, for deep-frying
a chilli sauce, to serve

MAKES 40

USING a food processor or blender, whiz the prawns, chicken or pork to a fine paste. In a bowl, combine the minced prawn or meat, water chestnuts, garlic, spring onions, oyster sauce, white pepper and salt.

TO MAKE spring onion ties, cut each into 4 to 6 strips, using only the longest green parts, then soak them in boiling water for 5 minutes or until soft. Drain, then dry on paper towels.

MIX the flour and 8 tablespoons cold water in a small saucepan until smooth. Stir and cook over a medium heat for 1 to 2 minutes or until thick.

PLACE 3 spring roll sheets in front of you and keep the remaining sheets in the plastic bag to prevent them drying out. Spoon 2 teaspoons of filling into the middle of each sheet. Brush around the filling with flour paste, then pull up into a bag and pinch together to enclose the filling. Place on a tray that is lightly dusted with plain (all-purpose) flour. Repeat until you have used all the filling and sheets. Tie a piece of spring onion twice around each bag and tie in a knot. Use chives if you prefer.

HEAT 7.5 cm (3 inches) oil in a wok or deep frying pan over a medium heat. When the oil seems hot, drop a small piece of spring roll sheet into it. If it sizzles immediately, the oil is ready. It is important not to have the oil too hot or the gold bags will cook too quickly and brown. Lower four bags into the oil and deep-fry for 2 to 3 minutes until they start to go hard. Lower another three or four bags into the oil and deep-fry them all together. To help cook the tops, splash the oil over the tops and deep-fry for 7 to 10 minutes or until golden and crispy. As each batch is cooked, lift the bags out with a slotted spoon and add another batch. Drain on paper towels. Keep the gold bags warm while deep-frying the rest. Serve with a chilli sauce.

## KHAO PHOHT THAWT
# SWEET CORN CAKES

400 g (2 cups) corn kernels
1 egg
3 tablespoons rice flour
1 tablespoon yellow curry paste
  (page 275)
2 tablespoons chopped Asian
  shallots
1 tablespoon fish sauce
25 g (½ cup) roughly chopped
  coriander (cilantro)
1 large red chilli, chopped
peanut oil, for shallow-frying
cucumber relish (page 287), to serve

MAKES 8

COMBINE the corn kernels, egg, rice flour, curry paste, shallots, fish sauce, coriander and chilli in a bowl. Shape the mixture into small patties, adding more rice flour, if necessary, to combine into a soft mixture.

HEAT the oil and fry the corn cakes for 3 to 4 minutes, turning once, until golden brown. Serve hot with cucumber relish.

Akah girl.

## KHANOM BANG NA KUNG
# SESAME PRAWNS ON TOASTS

280 g (10 oz) raw prawns (shrimp),
  peeled and deveined
2 teaspoons light soy sauce
1 egg
4–5 large garlic cloves,
  roughly chopped
7–8 coriander (cilantro) roots,
  roughly chopped
¼ teaspoon ground white pepper
½ teaspoon salt
7 slices day-old white bread,
  crusts removed, each slice
  cut into two triangles
3 tablespoons sesame seeds
peanut oil, for deep-frying
cucumber relish (page 287), to serve

MAKES 14

USING a food processor or blender, whiz the prawns into a smooth paste. Transfer to a bowl, add the light soy sauce and egg and mix well. Leave for about 30 minutes to firm.

USING a pestle and mortar, pound the garlic, coriander roots, white pepper and salt into a smooth paste. Add to the prawns. (Using a pestle and mortar gives the best texture but you can also whiz the garlic, coriander roots, pepper, light soy sauce and egg with the prawns.) Heat the grill (broiler) to medium. Spread the bread on a baking tray and put under the grill for 3 to 4 minutes or until the bread is dry and slightly crisp. Spread the prawn paste thickly on one side of each piece. Sprinkle with sesame seeds and press on firmly. Refrigerate for 30 minutes.

HEAT the oil in a wok or deep frying pan over a medium heat. Drop in a small cube of bread. If it sizzles immediately, the oil is ready. Deep-fry a few toasts at a time, paste-side down, for 3 minutes or until golden. Turn with a slotted spoon. Drain paste-side up on paper towels. Serve with relish.

SESAME PRAWNS ON TOASTS

Keep the spring roll sheets in their plastic bag so they don't dry out while you are rolling the rest.

# SPRING ROLLS

THESE SAVOURY ROLLS ARE POPULAR THROUGHOUT SOUTH-EAST ASIA. THE THAI VERSION IS A DELICATE CROSS BETWEEN CHINESE AND VIETNAMESE STYLES. THAI SPRING ROLLS ARE DEEP-FRIED UNTIL LIGHT GOLDEN BROWN AND CRISPY. THEY CAN BE SERVED WITH CHILLI OR LIGHT SOY SAUCE.

50 g (2 oz) vermicelli, cellophane
   or wun sen noodles
15 g (½ oz) dried black fungus
   (about half a handful)
2 tablespoons plain (all-purpose)
   flour
1½ tablespoons vegetable oil
3–4 garlic cloves, finely chopped
100 g (3½ oz) minced (ground)
   chicken or pork
1 small carrot, finely grated
140 g (1⅔ cups) bean sprouts
1 cm (½ inch) piece of ginger,
   finely grated
1½–2 tablespoons fish sauce
1½ tablespoons oyster sauce
¼ teaspoon ground white pepper
25 spring roll sheets 13 cm
   (5 inches) square
peanut oil, for deep-frying
a chilli sauce, to serve

MAKES 25 SMALL SPRING ROLLS

SOAK the vermicelli in hot water for 1 to 2 minutes or until soft. Drain, then cut into small pieces. Soak the dried mushrooms in hot water for 2 to 3 minutes or until soft. Drain, then finely chop. To make a paste, stir the flour and 2 tablespoons of water together in a small bowl until smooth.

HEAT the oil in a wok or frying pan and stir-fry the garlic until golden brown. Add the chicken or pork and using a spoon, break the meat until it separates into small bits and is cooked. Add the vermicelli, mushrooms, carrot, bean sprouts, ginger, fish sauce, oyster sauce and white pepper. Cook for another 4 to 5 minutes. Taste, then adjust the seasoning. Allow to cool.

PLACE 3 spring roll sheets on a work surface and spread some flour paste around the edges. Keep the remaining sheets in the plastic bag. Spoon 2 teaspoons of filling onto a sheet along the side nearest to you, about 2.5 cm (1 inch) from the edge. Bring the edge up, then roll it away from you a half turn over the filling. Fold the sides into the centre to enclose the filling, then wrap and seal the join tightly with the flour paste. Repeat with the rest of the filling and wrappers. (At this stage, the rolls can be frozen. If freezing, wrap each roll with another spring roll sheet.)

HEAT 5 cm (2 inches) oil in a wok or deep frying pan over a medium heat. When the oil seems hot, drop a small piece of spring roll sheet into the oil. If it sizzles immediately, the oil is ready. Don't have the oil too hot. Lower five rolls into the oil and deep-fry for 2 to 3 minutes. When they start to go hard, lower another four rolls into the oil and deep-fry them all together. To help cook the tops, splash oil over the tops. Deep-fry for 6 to 8 minutes or until crispy. As the spring rolls cook, lift out one at a time with a slotted spoon and add another. Drain on paper towels. Serve with a chilli sauce.

# CHICKEN WRAPPED IN PANDANUS LEAF

PANDANUS LEAVES ACT AS BOTH A WRAPPING AND A FLAVOURING IN THIS DISH. LEAVING A LONG TAIL ON THE PARCELS WILL MAKE THEM PRETTIER AND EASIER TO HANDLE SO DON'T TRIM THE LEAVES. TO EAT, CAREFULLY UNWRAP THE PARCELS AND DIP THE CHICKEN IN THE SAUCE.

5 coriander (cilantro) roots, cleaned
 and roughly chopped
4–5 garlic cloves
1 teaspoon ground white pepper
¼ teaspoon salt
600 g (1 lb 5 oz) skinless chicken
 breast fillets, cut into 25 cubes
2 tablespoons oyster sauce
1½ tablespoons sesame oil
1 tablespoon plain (all-purpose) flour
25 pandanus leaves, cleaned
 and dried
vegetable oil, for deep-frying
plum sauce (page 284) or a chilli
 sauce, to serve

MAKES 25

Pandanus leaves are used
to enclose the chicken in an
attractive tie shape.

USING a pestle and mortar or a small blender, pound or blend the coriander roots, garlic, white pepper and salt into a paste.

IN a bowl, combine the paste with the chicken, oyster sauce, sesame oil and flour. Cover with plastic wrap and marinate in the refrigerator for at least 3 hours, or overnight.

FOLD one of the pandanus leaves, bringing the base up in front of the tip, making a cup. Put a piece of chicken in the fold and, moving the bottom of the leaf, wrap it around to create a tie and enclose the chicken. Repeat until you have used all the chicken.

HEAT the oil in a wok or deep frying pan over a medium heat.

WHEN the oil seems hot, drop a small piece of leaf into it. If it sizzles immediately, the oil is ready. Lower some parcels into the oil and deep-fry for 7 to 10 minutes or until the parcels feel firm. Lift out with a slotted spoon and drain on paper towels. Keep the cooked ones warm while deep-frying the rest. Transfer to a serving plate. Serve with plum sauce or a chilli sauce.

KUNG HOM PAR

# PRAWNS IN A BLANKET

THESE PRAWNS, WHICH ARE PREPARED IN CHINESE STYLE, ARE AN APPEALING CANAPE. CHOOSE PLUMP BIG PRAWNS AND LEAVE THE TAILS ON FOR ATTRACTIVE PRESENTATION. YOU CAN MARINATE THE PRAWNS OVERNIGHT IN THE REFRIGERATOR IF YOU WANT TO PREPARE AHEAD.

12 raw large prawns (shrimp), peeled and deveined, tails intact
1 tablespoon plain (all-purpose) flour
2 garlic cloves, roughly chopped
3 coriander (cilantro) roots, finely chopped
1 cm (½ inch) piece of ginger, roughly sliced
1½ tablespoons oyster sauce or, for a hotter flavour, ½ teaspoon red curry paste (page 276)
a sprinkle of ground white pepper
12 frozen spring roll sheets or filo sheets, 12 cm (5 inches) square, defrosted
peanut oil, for deep-frying
a chilli sauce, or plum sauce (page 284), to serve

SERVES 4

TO make the prawns easier to wrap, you can make 3 or 4 shallow incisions in the underside of each, then open up the cuts to straighten the prawns.

MIX the flour and 3 tablespoons water in a small saucepan until smooth. Stir and cook over a medium heat for 1 to 2 minutes or until thick. Remove from the heat.

USING a pestle and mortar or a small blender, pound or blend the garlic, coriander roots and ginger together.

IN a bowl, combine the garlic paste with the prawns, oyster sauce, pepper and a pinch of salt. Cover with plastic wrap and marinate in the refrigerator for 2 hours, turning occasionally.

PLACE a spring roll or filo sheet on the work surface and keep all the remaining sheets in the plastic bag to prevent them drying out. Fold the sheet in half, remove a prawn from the marinade and place it on the sheet with its tail sticking out of the top. Fold the bottom up and then the sides in to tightly enclose the prawn. Seal the joins tightly with the flour paste. Repeat with the rest of the prawns and wrappers.

HEAT the oil in a wok or deep frying pan over a medium heat. When the oil seems hot, drop a small piece of spring roll sheet into it. If it sizzles immediately, the oil is ready. Deep-fry four prawns at a time for 3 to 4 minutes or until golden brown and crispy. Remove with a slotted spoon and drain on paper towels. Keep the prawns warm while deep-frying the rest.

TRANSFER to a serving plate. Serve hot with chilli sauce or plum sauce.

Large prawns are best for making these little bites. The attractive tails make them easier to pick up.

Sausages are a popular snack.

PORK SAUSAGES

KUNG PHAT BAI PHAK CHII LAE PHRIK

## PRAWNS WITH CORIANDER LEAVES AND CHILLI

350 g (12 oz) raw prawns (shrimp)
1 garlic clove, finely chopped
1 tablespoon coriander (cilantro)
   leaves, finely chopped
½–1 long red chilli, seeded and
   finely chopped
2 teaspoons lime juice
2 teaspoons vegetable oil
1 teaspoon sesame oil
1½ teaspoons light soy sauce
1 tablespoon oyster sauce
¼ teaspoon ground white pepper
4 bamboo sticks

SERVES 4

PEEL and devein the prawns and cut each prawn along the back so it opens like a butterfly (leave each prawn joined along the base and at the tail).

PUT the garlic, coriander, chilli, lime juice, both oils, light soy sauce, oyster sauce and ground pepper in a shallow dish and mix well. Add the prawns to the marinade and mix to coat the prawns. Cover with plastic wrap and marinate in the refrigerator for at least 30 minutes, or overnight.

SOAK the bamboo sticks in water for 1 hour to help prevent them from burning during cooking. Thread the prawns onto the skewers.

HEAT a barbecue or grill (broiler) to a high heat. If using a grill, line the tray with foil. Grill (broil) the prawns a good distance below the high heat for 8 to 10 minutes on each side. If you cook them directly on a barbecue plate they will cook more quickly, about 4 to 5 minutes. Turn the prawn sticks frequently until the prawns turn pink and are cooked through. You can brush the marinade sauce over the prawns during the cooking. Serve hot.

SAI UA

## PORK SAUSAGES

THIS KIND OF PORK SAUSAGE IS USUALLY ENCASED IN SKIN. HOWEVER, THIS RECIPE WITHOUT SKIN IS MUCH EASIER. IN THAILAND SOME SAUSAGES ARE LEFT TO FERMENT BEFORE COOKING BUT THEY TASTE JUST AS GOOD WHEN FRESH. SERVE WITH RAW VEGETABLES SUCH AS CABBAGE WEDGES.

3 coriander (cilantro) roots
1 lemon grass stalk, white part only,
   chopped
4 garlic cloves, chopped
½ teaspoon ground white pepper
1 small red chilli, chopped
2 teaspoons fish sauce
2 teaspoons sugar
300 g (10 oz) minced (ground) pork

SERVES 4

USING a pestle and mortar or food processor, pound or blend the coriander, lemon grass, garlic and pepper to a fine paste.

ADD the chilli, fish sauce, sugar and pork to the paste mixture and combine well. Form into sausage shapes.

HEAT a barbecue or grill (broiler) and cook the sausages for 4 to 5 minutes each side until cooked through.

# SON-IN-LAW EGGS

A TRADITIONAL CELEBRATION DISH, THESE EGGS ARE ENJOYED ON NEW YEAR'S DAY OR AT WEDDING FEASTS, AND ARE TAKEN AS AN OFFERING TO THE MONKS WHEN THAI PEOPLE VISIT THEIR LOCAL TEMPLE. THEY MAKE GOOD SNACKS. DEEP-FRYING GIVES THE SKINS A UNIQUE TEXTURE.

2 dried long red chillies, about
  13 cm (5 inches) long
vegetable oil, for deep-frying
110 g (4 oz) Asian shallots,
  finely sliced
6 large hard-boiled eggs, shelled
2 tablespoons fish sauce
3 tablespoons tamarind purée
5 tablespoons palm sugar

SERVES 4

CUT the chillies into 5 mm (¼ inch) pieces with scissors or a knife and discard the seeds. Heat 5 cm (2 inches) oil in a wok or deep frying pan over a medium heat. When the oil seems hot, drop a slice of the Asian shallot into the oil. If it sizzles straight away, the oil is ready. Deep-fry the chillies for a few seconds, being careful not to burn them, to bring out the flavour. Remove them with a slotted spoon, then drain on paper towels.

IN the same wok, deep-fry the Asian shallots for 3 to 4 minutes until golden brown. Be careful not to burn them. Remove with a slotted spoon, then drain on paper towels. Use a spoon to slide one egg at a time into the same hot oil. Be careful as the oil may splash. Deep-fry for 10 to 15 minutes or until the whole of each egg is golden brown. Remove with a slotted spoon, then drain on paper towels. Keep warm.

IN a saucepan over a medium heat, stir the fish sauce, tamarind purée and sugar for 5 to 7 minutes or until all the sugar has dissolved.

HALVE the eggs lengthways and arrange them with the yolk upwards on a serving plate. Drizzle the tamarind sauce over the eggs and sprinkle the crispy chillies and shallots over them.

When the eggs are golden, they are ready. Carefully remove with a slotted spoon and drain on paper towels.

MIANG KHAM

# BETEL LEAVES WITH SAVOURY TOPPING

2 tablespoons peanut oil
4 Asian shallots, finely sliced
2 garlic cloves, smashed with the
    side of a cleaver
150 g (5 oz) minced (ground)
    chicken or pork
2 tablespoons fish sauce
1 tablespoon tamarind purée
1 tablespoon dried shrimp, chopped
2 tablespoons palm sugar
1 cm (½ inch) piece of ginger, grated
2 bird's eye chillies, finely chopped
1 tablespoon roasted peanuts,
    chopped
1 tablespoon chopped coriander
    (cilantro) leaves
16 betel leaves
lime wedges, for squeezing

MAKES 16

HEAT the oil in a wok and fry the shallots and garlic for a minute or two until they brown. Add the chicken and fry it until the meat turns opaque, breaking up any lumps with the back of a spoon. Add the fish sauce, tamarind purée, shrimp and palm sugar and cook everything together until the mixture is brown and sticky. Stir in the ginger, chillies, peanuts and coriander leaves.

LAY the betel leaves out on a large plate and top each with some of the mixture. Serve with the lime wedges to squeeze over the mixture.

GALLOPING HORSES

MAR HOR

# GALLOPING HORSES

1½ tablespoons vegetable oil
2–3 garlic cloves, finely chopped
225 g (8 oz) minced (ground) pork
1 spring onion (scallion), finely sliced
½ tablespoon coriander (cilantro)
    leaves, finely chopped
25 g (1 oz) unsalted cooked
    peanuts, roughly ground
2 tablespoons light soy sauce
3 tablespoons palm sugar
a pinch of ground white pepper
16 small segments of pineapple,
    or tangerine, mandarin
    or orange segments
a few coriander (cilantro) leaves,
    for garnish
1 red chilli, very finely sliced,
    for garnish

SERVES 4

HEAT the oil in a saucepan or wok and stir-fry the garlic until golden brown. Add the pork and cook over a medium heat. With a spoon, break up the meat until it has separated and is almost dry. Add the spring onion, coriander leaves, ground peanuts, light soy sauce, sugar and pepper. Stir together for 4 to 5 minutes or until the mixture is dry and sticky.

IF YOU are using pineapple, spoon some mixture onto each segment.

IF USING citrus fruit, cut each segment from top to bottom, around the outer curve, and open each up like a butterfly. Remove any pips.

ARRANGE the segments on a serving plate and, with a teaspoon, transfer a little pork mixture onto each piece. Place a coriander leaf and a slice of chilli on top of each.

HAWY THAWT

# FRIED MUSSEL PANCAKE

2 kg (4 lb 8 oz) large mussels
   in their shells (yielding around
   350 g/12 oz meat)

CHILLI SAUCE
1 long red chilli, seeded and
   finely chopped
2½ tablespoons white vinegar
½ teaspoon sugar

50 g (2 oz) tapioca or plain
   (all-purpose) flour
40 g (⅓ cup) cornflour (cornstarch)
1 tablespoon fish sauce
1 teaspoon sugar
6 garlic cloves, finely chopped
350 g (4 cups) bean sprouts
4 spring onions (scallions), sliced
8 tablespoons vegetable oil
4 large eggs
a few coriander (cilantro) leaves
1 long red chilli, seeded and
   finely sliced
a sprinkle of ground white pepper
4 lime wedges

SERVES 4

SCRUB the mussels and remove their hairy beards. Discard any open mussels and any that don't close when tapped on the work surface. Preheat the oven to 180°C/350°F/Gas 4. Spread the mussels over a baking tray and bake for 5 minutes or until the shells open slightly. Discard any unopened mussels. When the shells return to a comfortable temperature, prise them open, scoop out the meat from each and put it in a colander to drain out out any juices.

TO MAKE the chilli sauce, mix the chilli, vinegar, sugar and a pinch of salt in a small serving bowl.

COMBINE the flours with 6 to 8 tablespoons water using a fork or spoon until the mixture is smooth and without lumps. Add the fish sauce and sugar. Divide among four bowls and add some mussels to each bowl.

SEPARATE the garlic, bean sprouts and spring onions into equal portions for each serving.

MAKE one pancake at a time. Heat 1 tablespoon oil in a small frying pan and stir-fry one portion of garlic over a medium heat until golden brown. Stir one portion of the mussel mixture with a spoon and pour it into the frying pan, swirling the pan to ensure that the mixture spreads evenly. Cook for 2 to 3 minutes or until it is brown underneath. Turn with a spatula and brown the other side. Make a hole in the centre and break an egg into the hole. Sprinkle a half portion of bean sprouts and spring onion over the top. Cook until the egg sets, then flip the pancake again. Turn the pancake onto a serving plate.

SPRINKLE each pancake with coriander leaves, sliced chilli and ground pepper. Place a lime wedge, bean sprouts and spring onions on the plate. Serve with the chilli sauce.

Choose small black mussels for these pancakes rather than the large green-lipped variety.

อาหารตามสั่ง

หมูแดงราดข้าว

# ข้าวผัด

ปู-กุ้ง-หมู-เนื้อ-ไก่ - 20.
ข้าวผัดพริกแกง - 20.
ข้าวผัดกะเพรา - 20.
ข้าวไก่ผัดเม็ดมะม่วง - 20.
ข้าวปูผงกะหรี่ - 20.
ข้าวผัดเปรี้ยวหวาน - 20

**STREET STALLS** Virtually every dish in Thai cuisine can be bought from one type of stall or another, the exception being royal cuisine. From full-blown meals, often a choice of two or three dishes with rice (top left) to simple snacks like grilled bananas (bottom left), mussel pancakes (centre) and satay (right) can be bought at any time of the day or night. Dishes like curries are pre-cooked but everything else is freshly made.

# STREET FOOD

THAIS LIKE TO EAT AT ALL HOURS OF THE DAY. STREET OR HAWKER FOOD IS A SUBCULTURE THAT THRIVES ALL OVER THE COUNTRY. *ROT KHEN* (VENDOR CARTS) ARE PARKED BY THE ROADSIDE IN EVEN THE SMALLEST VILLAGE. MOSTLY FOUND NEAR MARKETS DURING THE DAY, HAWKER FOOD COMES INTO ITS OWN AT DUSK AND INTO THE NIGHT.

## WHERE TO FIND STREET FOOD

Hawker stalls are allowed to set up virtually wherever they like. They can be found around the edge of markets, beside busy roads, down back streets or close to bus stops and stations. Stalls can be simple carts, which are pushed home every night, or they can be more permanent. Those that have a good reputation last for years, decades, and even generations on the same spot.

## TYPES OF STREET FOOD

There are five basic types of street food identifiable by the type of stall that sells them. Look out for the right type of cart and it will have the dish you are looking for. Carts with glass showcases sell dishes like *som tam* (green papaya salad),

Pieces of roast pork are popular (top left), sold with two types of dipping sauce. Corn on the cob (top right) is a relatively new introduction. Corn grows in areas where rice can't be cultivated. Chinese-style soups are popular at lunchtime (bottom left) and insects of various types, such as these deep-fried cockroaches with a chilli dipping sauce (bottom right), are common in the northern part of Thailand.

noodle dishes and soups, roast pork and chicken and Chinese chicken rice. Stalls with charcoal barbecues sell satay, barbecued chicken and pork, Thai sausages, dried squid and grilled bananas. Steamer domes indicate red braised pork, Chinese dumplings and buns, pumpkin custard and sticky rice in banana leaves. Carts fitted with a large hotplate make mussels in batter, omelettes, pancakes and fried noodles. Woks mean spring rolls, won tons, fish cakes and dough sticks. Ready-cooked food comes from vendors with prepared dishes such as fish curry in banana cups, pork-rind soups and lots of different puddings such as sticky rice. Drinks carts sell fruit juices and sweets served over crushed ice. Other specialist carts sell fresh fruit, preserved fruit and seafood, including boiled clams or cockles.

## PALM SUGAR PARCELS

**PALM SUGAR AND PEANUT PARCELS** These steamed sweet snacks are made by wrapping peanut paste in a flour and sugar paste and then spooning the filling into banana leaves. Deft hands and plenty of practice are needed to fold the banana leaves into neat triangles before steaming them in a large steamer. The vendor makes the same amount of parcels daily and keeps the stall open until everything sells out.

## SOM TAM

**MAKING SOM TAM** Not quite a salad and not quite anything else either, *som tam* is made in single portions and served as a snack with sticky rice. The bulk of the dish is green papaya that has been finely shredded, to which tomatoes, palm sugar, peanuts, chilli and lime juice, fish sauce, dried prawns, garlic, snake beans and herbs are added. The customer tastes the *som tam* and adjusts the flavour as it is made.

## ROTI

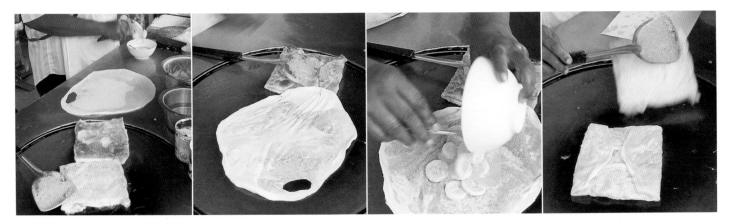

**MAKING BANANA ROTI** Roti are Indian-style pastries that are cooked on a flat hotplate. The name means bread but the finished dish resembles a pancake or pastry rather than anything doughy. The roti are made by spreading a fine, stretchy dough on a hotplate and then adding sweet fillings like bananas and condensed milk and folding the dough over them. The result is a crispy pastry with a soft, sweet filling.

**NOODLE SOUP** Noodles are generally sold as a snack in Thailand. These are *khanom jiin*, rice noodles, made in the North-Eastern style, served with fennel.

**BARBECUED CHICKEN** Roadside rotisseries provide a constant supply of chickens cooked over charcoal. They are chopped into pieces on request.

**DRIED SQUID** Grilled dried squid is a popular night-time snack in Thailand. The dried squid are rolled to soften them before they are grilled over hot coals.

**THAI SAUSAGES** Spicy pork sausages are very popular in Thailand. These are made from pork with glutinous rice and seasonings and are sold grilled.

**FRIED FISH** Fish are eaten all over Thailand and are often fried whole. They are commonly served over rice with a chilli sauce of some sort.

**THAI OLIVES** This is a snack sold in small plastic bags, along with a seasoning of chilli sugar, combining opposing flavours, which is common in Thailand.

**GRILLED BANANAS** Eaten in many ways, small sugar bananas are often grilled over coals until the outside browns and the inside is soft, then eaten as a snack.

**STEAMED STICKY RICE** Steamed sticky rice wrapped in banana leaves has added flavourings such as coconut, mashed taro or black beans.

**COCONUT PUDDINGS** These are made by pouring batter and sweet coconut milk into a mould, sometimes with flavouring, then baking over charcoal or gas.

**DEEP-FRIED PORK BELLY** Large pieces of this pork are cut into slices and sold with little bags of chilli dipping sauce. Smaller pieces are fried as they are.

**CHINESE-STYLE SOUP** *(kaeng jeut)*, or bland soup, is steamed in individual bowls. Soups are eaten with meals except, as here, when a snack.

**CHINESE STEAMED BUNS** A fluffy dough is filled with barbecued or minced pork, or yellow mung beans, to make a Chinese dim sum speciality.

SOUPS

The delicious flavour of this soup comes from the melding of prawn, chicken and vegetables.

A huge woven basket used for threshing rice.

KHAO TOM KUNG LAE KAI

# RICE SOUP WITH PRAWNS AND CHICKEN

ALTHOUGH DERIVED FROM CHINESE-STYLE 'CONGEE, THAI RICE SOUPS USE WHOLE RICE GRAINS RATHER THAN THE BROKEN GRAINS PREFERRED BY THE CHINESE. RICE SOUPS ARE ENJOYED AS A SNACK AT NIGHT OR AS A BREAKFAST DISH. THEY ARE SUSTAINING ENOUGH TO BE A MEAL.

110 g (4 oz) raw prawns (shrimp)
2 tablespoons vegetable oil
3–4 large garlic cloves,
    finely chopped
1 coriander (cilantro) root,
    finely chopped
1 garlic clove, extra, roughly
    chopped
a pinch of ground white pepper,
    plus extra, to sprinkle
75 g (3 oz) minced (ground) chicken
    or pork
1 spring onion (scallion),
    finely chopped
935 ml (3¾ cups) chicken or
    vegetable stock
2 tablespoons light soy sauce
2 teaspoons preserved radish
325 g (1¾ cups) cooked jasmine
    rice
1 tablespoon finely sliced ginger
1 Chinese cabbage leaf, roughly
    chopped
2 spring onions (scallions), finely
    chopped, for garnish
a few coriander (cilantro) leaves,
    for garnish

SERVES 4

PEEL and devein the prawns and cut each prawn along the back so it opens like a butterfly (leave each prawn joined along the base and at the tail, leaving the tail attached).

HEAT the oil in a small wok or frying pan and stir-fry the finely chopped garlic until light golden. Remove from the heat and discard the garlic.

USING a pestle and mortar or a small blender, pound or blend the coriander root, roughly chopped garlic, pepper and a pinch of salt into a paste. In a bowl, combine the coriander paste with the chicken or pork and spring onion. Using a spoon or your wet hands, shape the mixture into small balls about 1 cm (½ inch) across.

HEAT the stock to boiling point in a saucepan. Add the light soy sauce, preserved radish and rice. Lower the meatballs into the stock over a medium heat and cook for 3 minutes or until the chicken is cooked. Add the prawns, ginger and Chinese cabbage to the stock. Cook for another 1 to 2 minutes or until the prawns open and turn pink. Taste, then adjust the seasoning if necessary.

GARNISH with spring onions and coriander leaves. Sprinkle with ground white pepper and the garlic oil.

KAENG JEUT PLAA MEUK SAI MUU

# STUFFED SQUID SOUP

KAENG JEUT ARE ONE OF THE THREE MAIN TYPES OF SOUP COMMONLY FOUND IN THAILAND. THE NAME MEANS BLAND SOUP. THIS SOUP IS ANOTHER THAI DISH WITH A CHINESE INFLUENCE. THESE SOUPS ARE NOT HIGHLY FLAVOURED SO YOU SHOULD USE THE BEST QUALITY STOCK POSSIBLE.

280 g (10 oz) small squid

2 coriander (cilantro) roots, finely chopped

3–4 large garlic cloves, roughly chopped

280 g (10 oz) minced (ground) pork or chicken

¼ teaspoon salt

¼ teaspoon ground white pepper

2 litres (8 cups) vegetable stock

2.5 cm (1 inch) piece of ginger, sliced

4 tablespoons light soy sauce

1 tablespoon preserved radish, sliced

5 spring onions (scallions), slivered, for garnish

a few coriander (cilantro) leaves, for garnish

ground white pepper, for sprinkling

SERVES 4

TO CLEAN each squid, grasp the squid body in one hand and pull away the head and tentacles from the body. Cut the head off the tentacles just above the eyes and discard the head. Clean out the body. Pull the skin off the squid and rinse well. Drain well.

USING a pestle and mortar, pound the coriander roots and garlic into a paste. In a bowl, combine the coriander paste with the pork or chicken and the salt and pepper. Spoon some mixture into a squid sac until two-thirds full, being careful not to overfill it as the filling will swell during cooking. Squeeze the squid tube closed at the end. With a bamboo stick or sharp toothpick, prick several holes in the body of the squid. Place on a plate and repeat with the rest. Use a spoon or your wet fingers to shape the remaining meat mixture into small balls about 1 cm (½ inch) across.

HEAT the stock to boiling point in a saucepan. Reduce the heat to low and add the ginger, light soy sauce and preserved radish. Lower the meatballs into the stock, then gently drop in the stuffed squid and cook over a low heat for 4 to 5 minutes or until the meatballs and squid are cooked. Taste the broth and adjust the seasoning if necessary.

GARNISH with spring onions and coriander leaves. Sprinkle with ground white pepper.

Don't stuff too much of the mixture into the squid sac as it will swell during cooking.

Soup flavourings are often sold ready-made in bundles.

It is best to carefully measure ingredients such as fish sauce as the flavour is quite strong.

# CHICKEN, COCONUT AND GALANGAL SOUP

THIS IS ONE OF THE CLASSIC SOUPS OF THAILAND. THE THAI NAME MEANS 'BOILED GALANGAL CHICKEN'. ALTHOUGH USUALLY MADE WITH CHICKEN, YOU CAN MAKE THIS RECIPE USING PRAWNS, FISH OR VEGETABLES. DON'T WORRY WHEN THE COCONUT MILK SPLITS — IT IS SUPPOSED TO.

750 ml (3 cups) coconut milk
  (page 279)
2 lemon grass stalks, white part
  only, each cut into a tassel
  or bruised
5 cm (2 inch) piece of galangal,
  cut into several pieces
4 Asian shallots, smashed with
  the flat side of a cleaver
400 g (14 oz) skinless chicken
  breast fillets, cut into slices
2 tablespoons fish sauce
1 tablespoon palm sugar
200 g (7 oz) baby tomatoes, cut
  into bite-sized pieces if large
150 g (5 oz) straw mushrooms
  or button mushrooms
3 tablespoons lime juice
6 makrut (kaffir) lime leaves,
  torn in half
3–5 bird's eye chillies, stems
  removed, bruised, or 2 long red
  chillies, seeded and finely sliced
a few coriander (cilantro) leaves,
  for garnish

SERVES 4

PUT the coconut milk, lemon grass, galangal and shallots in a saucepan or wok over a medium heat and bring to a boil.

ADD the chicken, fish sauce and palm sugar and simmer, stirring constantly for 5 minutes or until the chicken is cooked through.

ADD the tomatoes and mushrooms and simmer for 2 to 3 minutes. Add the lime juice, makrut lime leaves and chillies in the last few seconds, taking care not to let the tomatoes lose their shape. Taste, then adjust the seasoning if necessary. This dish is not meant to be overwhelmingly hot, but to have a sweet, salty, sour taste. Serve garnished with coriander leaves.

TOM YAM KUNG

# HOT AND SOUR PRAWN SOUP

THIS SOUP IS PROBABLY THE MOST WELL KNOWN THAI DISH OF ALL. ALTHOUGH IT IS USUALLY MADE WITH PRAWNS, IT WORKS EQUALLY WELL WITH FISH. TO ACHIEVE THE FAMOUS DISTINCTIVE AROMA AND FLAVOURS, USE ONLY THE FRESHEST GOOD-QUALITY INGREDIENTS.

350 g (12 oz) raw prawns (shrimp)
1 tablespoon oil
3 lemon grass stalks, white part
   only, bruised
3 thin slices of galangal
2 litres (8 cups) chicken stock
   or water
5–7 bird's eye chillies, stems
   removed, bruised
5 makrut (kaffir) lime leaves, torn
2 tablespoons fish sauce
70 g (2 oz) straw mushrooms,
   or quartered button mushrooms
2 spring onions (scallions), sliced
3 tablespoons lime juice
a few coriander (cilantro) leaves,
   for garnish

SERVES 4

PEEL and devein the prawns, leaving the tails intact and reserving the heads and shells. Heat the oil in a large stockpot or wok and add the prawn heads and shells. Cook for 5 minutes or until the shells turn bright orange.

ADD one stalk of lemon grass to the pan with the galangal and stock or water. Bring to the boil, then reduce the heat and simmer for 20 minutes. Strain the stock and return to the pan. Discard the shells and flavourings.

FINELY slice the remaining lemon grass and add it to the liquid with the chillies, lime leaves, fish sauce, mushrooms and spring onions. Cook gently for 2 minutes.

ADD the prawns and cook for 3 minutes or until the prawns are firm and pink. Take off the heat and add the lime juice. Taste, then adjust the seasoning with extra lime juice or fish sauce if necessary. Garnish with coriander leaves.

# VERMICELLI SOUP WITH MINCED PORK

THIS IS A LIGHT, CLEAR SOUP FROM THE NORTH OF THAILAND. UNLIKE OTHER NOODLE RECIPES THIS ONE IS ALWAYS EATEN WITH RICE. IT IS A WARMING 'COMFORT FOOD' AND IS VERY EASY TO PREPARE. THE NOODLES CONTINUE TO SOAK UP LIQUID AS THEY SIT, SO SERVE THE SOUP STRAIGHT AWAY.

15 pieces of dried black fungus
50 g (2 oz) mung bean vermicelli
2 tablespoons vegetable oil
3–4 large garlic cloves, finely
   chopped
450 g (1 lb) minced (ground) pork
20 coriander (cilantro) leaves,
   finely chopped
¼ teaspoon salt
¼ teaspoon ground white pepper
625 ml (2½ cups) vegetable or
   chicken stock
2 tablespoons light soy sauce
1 tablespoon preserved radish
a few coriander (cilantro) leaves,
   for garnish

SERVES 4

SOAK the mushrooms in hot water for 5 minutes or until soft, then drain them and cut into smaller pieces if necessary.

SOAK the mung bean vermicelli in hot water for 5 to 7 minutes or until soft, then drain it well and cut it into small pieces.

HEAT the oil in a small wok or frying pan and stir-fry the garlic until light golden. Remove from the heat, lift out the garlic with a slotted spoon and drain on paper towels.

IN a bowl, combine the pork with the coriander leaves, salt and pepper. Use a spoon or your wet hands to shape the mixture into small balls about 1 cm (½ inch) across.

HEAT the stock to boiling point in a saucepan. Add the light soy sauce and preserved radish. Lower the pork balls into the stock and cook for 2 minutes over a medium heat. Add the mushrooms and noodles and cook for another 1 to 2 minutes, stirring frequently. Taste, then adjust the seasoning if necessary. Sprinkle with crispy garlic, garlic oil and coriander leaves.

Pedal power competes with cars in Chiang Mai.

TOM YAM TAO-HUU

# FRAGRANT TOFU AND TOMATO SOUP

TOFU, OR BEAN CURD, COMES IN SEVERAL DIFFERENT VARIETIES, FROM SOFT TO QUITE FIRM. THE
SOFTEST, CALLED SILKEN TOFU, HAS THE BEST TYPE OF TEXTURE FOR THIS RECIPE. THE STRONG
FLAVOURINGS USED IN THE RECIPE ARE A PERFECT CONTRAST FOR THE TOFU.

PASTE
½ teaspoon dried shrimp paste
1 teaspoon small dried prawns
   (shrimp)
4 Asian shallots, roughly chopped
½ teaspoon white peppercorns
2 coriander (cilantro) roots
1 garlic clove, chopped
2 teaspoons grated ginger

1 tablespoon vegetable oil
750 ml (3 cups) chicken stock
   or water
3 tablespoons tamarind purée
1 tablespoon palm sugar
2 tablespoons fish sauce
3 cm (1¼ inch) piece of ginger,
   julienned
3 Asian shallots, smashed with the
   flat side of a cleaver
300 g (10 oz) silken tofu
   (bean curd), cut into 2 cm (¾ inch)
   cubes
2 tomatoes, each cut into 8 wedges
1 tablespoon lime juice
2 tablespoons coriander (cilantro)
   leaves, for garnish

SERVES 4

TO MAKE the paste, use a pestle and mortar or
food processor to pound or blend the shrimp
paste, dried prawns, shallots, peppercorns,
coriander roots, garlic and ginger together.

HEAT the oil in a saucepan over a low heat, add
the paste and cook for 10 to 15 seconds, stirring
constantly. Add the stock or water, tamarind
purée, palm sugar, fish sauce and ginger. Simmer
for 5 minutes to soften the ginger.

ADD the shallots, tofu, tomatoes and lime juice to
the pan and cook for 2 to 3 minutes to heat
through. Garnish with coriander leaves.

Pound the ingredients in a pestle and mortar to make a paste, then mix with the chicken and shape into small balls.

# VEGETABLE SOUP WITH CHICKEN AND PRAWN

A BLAND SOUP THAT IS BEST SERVED WITH A MEAL, TO BE EATEN ALONGSIDE THE OTHER MAIN DISHES. BLAND SOUPS HELP TAKE THE HEAT OUT OF CHILLI DISHES. THE CHICKEN BALLS IN THIS SOUP ARE EASILY MADE BUT YOU COULD USE CUBES OF CHICKEN INSTEAD. USE GOOD-QUALITY STOCK.

175 g (6 oz) raw prawns (shrimp)
2 coriander (cilantro) roots, cleaned
  and finely chopped
2 garlic cloves, roughly chopped
pinch of ground white pepper,
  plus extra, to sprinkle
150 g (5 oz) minced (ground)
  chicken
½ spring onion (scallion), finely
  chopped
935 ml (3¾ cups) chicken or
  vegetable stock
2 tablespoons light soy sauce
2 teaspoons preserved radish
175 g (6 oz) marrow or pumpkin
  (squash), cut into 2.5 cm (1 inch)
  cubes
175 g (6 oz) Chinese cabbage,
  roughly chopped
a few coriander (cilantro) leaves,
  for garnish

SERVES 4

PEEL and devein the prawns and cut each prawn along the back so it opens like a butterfly (leave each prawn joined along the base and at the tail, leaving the tail attached).

USING a pestle and mortar or a small blender, pound or blend the coriander roots, garlic, pepper and a pinch of salt into a paste. In a bowl, combine the coriander paste with the chicken and spring onion. Use a spoon or your wet hands to shape the chicken mixture into small balls about 1 cm (½ inch) across.

HEAT the stock to boiling point in a saucepan. Add the light soy sauce and preserved radish. Lower the chicken balls into the stock and cook over a medium heat for 1 to 2 minutes or until the balls are cooked.

ADD the marrow to the pan and cook for 2 to 3 minutes. Add the prawns and Chinese cabbage and cook for another 1 to 2 minutes. Taste, then adjust the seasoning if necessary. Garnish with coriander leaves. Sprinkle with ground white pepper.

KAENG SOM PLA KUP PHAK BUNG

# SOUR FISH SOUP WITH WATER SPINACH

THIS SOUP IS A POPULAR ADDITION TO A MAIN MEAL IN THAILAND. YOU CAN SUBSTITUTE MEAT FOR THE FISH IF YOU PREFER. WATER SPINACH IS ALSO KNOWN AS MORNING GLORY AND ONG CHOY.

SOUR CURRY PASTE
3 garlic cloves, roughly chopped
3 bird's eye chillies, stems removed
1 Asian shallot, chopped
1 teaspoon grated galangal
1 teaspoon grated turmeric
   (or a pinch of dried)
1 teaspoon shrimp paste

175 g (6 oz) skinless white fish fillets
3 tablespoons tamarind purée
175 g (6 oz) water spinach, cut into
   pieces, leaves separated
1 tablespoon fish sauce
1 tablespoon sugar

SERVES 4

TO MAKE the sour curry paste, use a pestle and mortar or food processor to pound or blend all the ingredients together until smooth.

REMOVE any remaining bones from the fish using tweezers, then cut the fish fillets into 5 cm (2 inch) pieces.

IN a saucepan, bring 625 ml (2½ cups) water to the boil. Stir in the sour curry paste and reduce the heat to medium. Add the tamarind, water spinach stems, fish sauce and sugar and cook for 2 to 3 minutes. Add the fish fillets and cook for another 1 to 2 minutes. Add the water spinach leaves and gently mix. Taste, then adjust the seasoning if necessary. Spoon into a serving bowl and serve hot with rice.

KHAO TOM PLAA

# RICE SOUP WITH FISH FILLET

RICE SOUP WITH FISH FILLET

2 tablespoons vegetable oil
3–4 large garlic cloves, finely chopped
1.25 litres (5 cups) vegetable,
   chicken or fish stock
2½ tablespoons light soy sauce
2 teaspoons preserved radish,
   sliced
245 g (1⅓ cups) cooked jasmine
   rice
280 g (10 oz) skinless white fish
   fillets, cut into bite-sized pieces
1 tablespoon finely sliced ginger
1 spring onion (scallion), finely
   chopped, for garnish
a few coriander (cilantro) leaves,
   for garnish
ground white pepper, for sprinkling

SERVES 4

HEAT the oil in a small wok or frying pan and stir-fry the garlic until light golden. Remove from the heat and discard the garlic.

HEAT the stock to boiling point in a saucepan. Add the light soy sauce, preserved radish and rice and cook over a medium heat for 2 to 3 minutes. Add the fish and ginger and cook for another 1 to 2 minutes or until the fish is cooked. Season well, taste, then adjust the seasoning again if necessary.

GARNISH with spring onion and coriander leaves and sprinkle with ground pepper and the garlic oil.

# HOT AND SOUR SOUP WITH MIXED SEAFOOD

YOU CAN USE YOUR FAVOURITE COMBINATION OF SEAFOOD FOR THIS SOUP BUT MAKE SURE IT IS ALL ABSOLUTELY FRESH TO ENSURE A DELICIOUS TASTE. THE CURRY PASTE WILL MAKE THE SOUP BROTH CLOUDIER THAN IF USING DRIED CHILLIES BUT IT WILL RESULT IN A MORE COMPLEX FLAVOUR.

600 g (1 lb 5 oz) mixed fresh
    seafood such as raw prawns
    (shrimp), squid tubes, mussels,
    white fish fillets and scallops
1 litre (4 cups) vegetable stock
3 x 4 cm (1½ inch) lemon grass
    stalks, white part only, each cut
    into a tassel or bruised
6 coriander (cilantro) roots, bruised
2–2½ tablespoons fish sauce
1½–2 tablespoons Chiang Mai curry
    paste (page 272), according to
    taste, or 2 dried red chillies,
    soaked, drained and
    finely chopped
2–3 bird's eye chillies, bruised
2 Asian shallots, smashed with
    the flat side of a cleaver
110 g (4 oz) straw or mixed
    mushrooms, left whole if small,
    or quartered if large
150 g (5 oz) baby tomatoes (about
    12, cut in half if large) or medium
    tomatoes, each cut into 6 pieces
8 makrut (kaffir) lime leaves, torn
3 tablespoons lime juice

SERVES 4

PEEL and devein the prawns and cut each prawn along the back so it opens like a butterfly (leave each prawn joined along the base and at the tail).

PEEL off any skin from the squid tubes, rinse the insides and cut the tubes into 5 mm (¼ inch) rings. If the squid are very big, cut them in half, open the tubes and slightly score the inside of each squid with diagonal cuts to make a diamond pattern. Cut the tubes into pieces about 2 cm (¾ inch) square. Remove any dark veins from the scallops.

SCRUB the mussels and remove their hairy beards. Discard any open mussels and any that don't close when tapped on the work surface. Cut the fish into 2 cm (¾ inch) cubes.

PUT the stock, lemon grass, coriander roots, fish sauce, curry paste and chillies in a large saucepan and bring to a boil.

REDUCE the heat to medium, add the seafood and cook for 2 to 3 minutes. (If using cooked mussels, add them after the tomatoes.) Add the shallots, mushrooms, baby tomatoes, makrut lime leaves and cook for another 2 to 3 minutes, taking care not to let the tomatoes lose their shape. Taste, add the lime juice, then adjust the seasoning if necessary. Spoon into a serving bowl.

Put the lemon grass, coriander roots, fish sauce, curry paste, chillies and stock in the pan.

KAENG JEUT TAO-HUU SAI KUNG

# STUFFED TOFU SOUP WITH PRAWNS

THIS RECIPE IS QUITE FIDDLY BUT WELL WORTH THE EFFORT. DON'T OVERSTUFF THE TOFU OR IT MIGHT EXPLODE OUT AS IT COOKS. AS WITH OTHER 'BLAND' SOUPS, USE A GOOD-QUALITY STOCK. THE STUFFED TOFU CAN ALSO BE FRIED AND EATEN ON ITS OWN.

275 g (10 oz) raw prawns (shrimp)
2–3 coriander (cilantro) roots,
   roughly chopped
2 garlic cloves, roughly chopped
¼ teaspoon salt
1 tablespoon cornflour (cornstarch)
¼ teaspoon ground white pepper
320 g (11 oz) firm tofu (bean curd)
1.5 litres (6 cups) vegetable stock
2.5 cm (1 inch) piece of ginger,
   sliced
4 tablespoons light soy sauce
1 tablespoon preserved radish
5 spring onions (scallions), cut into
   slivers, for garnish

SERVES 4

PEEL and devein the prawns. Set aside about 80 g (3 oz) of the prawns and cut the rest of them along their backs so they open like a butterfly (leave each prawn joined along the base and at the tail).

USING a food processor or blender, whiz the coriander roots and garlic until as smooth as possible. Add the prawns that are not butterflied, along with the salt, cornflour and white pepper, then blend until as smooth as possible. If you prefer, you can use a pestle and mortar to pound the coriander roots and garlic into a paste before processing with the prawns. This gives a slightly better flavour.

Spoon some of the prepared prawn mixture into each tofu pocket, then carefully lower them into the stock.

DRAIN the tofu and cut it into 16 triangles. Cut a pocket into the long side of each piece of tofu with a knife. Spoon some prawn mixture into each pocket and gently press down on top. Repeat until you have used all the tofu and the mixture.

HEAT the stock to boiling point in a saucepan. Reduce the heat to low and add the ginger, light soy sauce and preserved radish. Lower the tofu envelopes into the stock and cook for 4 to 5 minutes or until cooked. Add the butterflied prawns and cook for another 1 to 2 minutes or until the prawns open and turn pink. Taste, then adjust the seasoning if necessary. Serve garnished with spring onions.

A spirit house in Damnoen Saduak.

SALADS

Slice off a section from the top of the pomelo before cutting it into sections and segmenting it.

# PRAWN AND POMELO SALAD

THIS NORTHERN THAI SALAD USES POMELO TO GIVE IT A SWEET/TART FLAVOUR. DIFFERENT VARIETIES OF POMELO ARE AVAILABLE IN THAILAND: SOME HAVE PINK FLESH AND OTHERS HAVE YELLOW. SERVE THE SALAD WITH STICKY RICE AND EAT IT AS SOON AS IT IS READY.

1 large pomelo
1 tablespoon fish sauce
1 tablespoon lime juice
1 teaspoon sugar
1 tablespoon chilli jam (page 283)
300 g (10 oz) raw medium prawns (shrimp), peeled and deveined, tails intact
3 tablespoons shredded fresh coconut, lightly toasted until golden (if fresh unavailable, use shredded desiccated)
3 Asian shallots, finely sliced
5 bird's eye chillies, bruised
20 g (1 cup) mint leaves
10 g (⅓ cup) coriander (cilantro) leaves
1 tablespoon fried Asian shallots

SERVES 4

TO PEEL a pomelo, first, slice a circular patch off the top of the fruit, about 2 cm (¾ inch) deep (roughly the thickness of the skin). Next, score four deep lines from top to bottom, dividing the skin into four segments. Peel away the skin, one quarter at a time. Remove any remaining pith and separate the segments of the fruit. Peel the segments and remove any seeds. Crumble the segments into their component parts, without squashing them or releasing the juice.

TO MAKE the dressing, combine the fish sauce, lime juice, sugar and chilli jam in a small bowl and stir.

BRING a large saucepan of water to the boil. Add the prawns and cook for 2 minutes. Drain and allow the prawns to cool.

IN a large bowl, gently combine the pomelo, prawns, toasted coconut, shallots, chillies, mint and coriander. Just before serving, add the dressing and toss gently to combine all the ingredients. Serve sprinkled with fried shallots.

Peeling pomelo in Pattaya.

YAM PLAA
# CRISPY FISH SALAD

THE FISH (TRADITIONALLY CATFISH) IN THIS RECIPE IS TURNED INTO AN ALMOST UNRECOGNIZABLE FLUFFY, CRUNCHY AFFAIR THAT IS THEN FLAVOURED WITH A SWEET, HOT AND SOUR DRESSING. PINK SALMON IS SUITABLE TO USE AS A SUBSTITUTE FOR THE WHITE FISH.

DRESSING
1 lemon grass stalk, white part
    only, roughly chopped
4 bird's eye chillies,
    stems removed
1 garlic clove, chopped
1 tablespoon fish sauce
2 tablespoons lime juice
2 teaspoons palm sugar
¼ teaspoon ground turmeric

300 g (10 oz) skinless firm white
    fish fillets
1 tablespoon sea salt
peanut oil, for deep-frying
3 tomatoes or large cherry
    tomatoes, each cut into
    4 or 6 wedges
2 Asian shallots, thinly sliced
1 small red onion, sliced into
    thin wedges
15 g (½ cup) coriander (cilantro)
    leaves
18–24 mint leaves
2 tablespoons roasted peanuts,
    roughly chopped

SERVES 4

TO MAKE the dressing, use a pestle and mortar or food processor to pound or blend the lemon grass, chillies and garlic to a paste. Transfer to a bowl and add the fish sauce, lime juice, sugar and turmeric. Stir until the sugar dissolves.

PREHEAT the oven to 180°C/350°F/Gas 4. Pat dry the fish fillets, then toss them in the sea salt. Place them on a rack in a baking tray and bake for 20 minutes. Remove, allow to cool, then transfer to a food processor and chop until the fish resembles large breadcrumbs.

HALF fill a wok with oil and heat over a high heat. Drop a small piece of fish into the oil. If it sizzles immediately, the oil is ready. Drop a large handful of the chopped fish into the hot oil. The fish will puff up and turn crisp. Cook for 30 seconds and carefully stir a little. Cook for another 30 seconds until golden brown. Remove with a slotted spoon and drain on paper towels. Repeat to cook all the fish.

PUT the tomatoes, shallots, red onion, coriander leaves, mint leaves and peanuts in a bowl with about half of the dressing. Transfer the salad to a serving plate. Break the fish into smaller pieces if you wish and place on the salad. To ensure that the fish stays crispy, pour the remaining dressing over the salad just before serving.

This tasty salad is made using a colourful combination with flavours that contrast well.

Pound the chilli paste ingredients together in a pestle and mortar, or if you prefer, use a blender.

YAM KAI

# CHICKEN AND PAPAYA SALAD

ONE OF THAILAND'S MANY HOT AND TANGY SALADS, THIS VERSION HAS COCONUT RICE INCLUDED, BUT YOU COULD SERVE IT ON ITS OWN IF YOU PREFER. MAKE SURE THE PAPAYA IS GREEN, AND NOT RIPE, OR THE SALAD WON'T TASTE AT ALL RIGHT.

250 ml (1 cup) coconut cream (page 279)
200 g (7 oz) skinless chicken breast fillet, trimmed
200 g (1 cup) jasmine rice
350 ml (1⅓ cups) coconut milk (page 279)
2 garlic cloves, chopped
3 Asian shallots, chopped
3 small red chillies
1 teaspoon small dried shrimp
2 tablespoons fish sauce
8 cherry tomatoes, cut in halves
150 g (5 oz) green papaya, grated
2 tablespoons lime juice
30 g (1½ cups) mint leaves, roughly chopped
20 g (⅔ cup) coriander (cilantro) leaves, roughly chopped

SERVES 4

BRING the coconut cream to a boil in a small saucepan. Add the chicken breast and simmer over a low heat for 5 minutes. Turn off the heat and cover the pan for 20 minutes. Remove the chicken from the pan and shred it.

WASH the rice under cold running water until the water runs clear. Put the rice and coconut milk in a small saucepan and bring to the boil. Reduce the heat to low, cover the pan with a tight-fitting lid and simmer for 20 minutes. Remove from the heat and leave the lid on until ready to serve.

USING a pestle and mortar or blender, pound or blend the garlic, shallots and chillies together. Add the shrimp and fish sauce and pound to break up the dried shrimp. Add the tomatoes and pound all the ingredients together to form a rough paste.

IN a bowl, combine the shredded chicken and chilli paste mixture with the grated papaya, lime juice, mint and coriander leaves. Serve with the hot coconut rice.

YAM HUA PLII
# SHREDDED CHICKEN AND BANANA BLOSSOM

BANANA BLOSSOMS LOOK LIKE VERY LARGE PURPLE FLOWER BUDS. MOST OF THE BLOSSOM IS
DISCARDED DURING PREPARATION AND ONLY THE SLIGHTLY BITTER CORE IS EATEN. THEY DISCOLOUR
IN SECONDS SO WORK QUICKLY OR YOU WILL END UP WITH BLACKENED SHREDS.

3 tablespoons lime juice
1 large banana blossom
250 ml (1 cup) coconut cream
  (page 279)
200 g (7 oz) skinless chicken breast
  fillet, trimmed
1 tablespoon chilli jam (page 283)
1 tablespoon fish sauce
1 tablespoon palm sugar
2 teaspoons lime juice
12 cherry tomatoes, cut in halves
20 g (1 cup) mint leaves
10 g (⅓ cup) coriander (cilantro)
  leaves
1 makrut (kaffir) lime leaf, finely
  shredded, for garnish

SERVES 4

PUT the lime juice in a large bowl of cold water.
Using a stainless steel knife, remove the outer
leaves of the banana blossom until you reach
the creamy pale centre. Cut the heart or centre
into quarters and remove the hard cores and
stamens from each. Finely slice the fleshy heart
on an angle and place the slices in the lime water
until ready to use.

RESERVE 2 tablespoons of the coconut cream
and pour the rest into a small saucepan and bring
to a boil. Add the chicken breast, return to a boil,
then reduce the heat and simmer for 5 minutes.
Remove from the heat and cover the pan with a
tight lid for 20 minutes. Remove the chicken from
the pan and discard the cream. Allow the chicken
to cool, then shred it into bite-sized pieces.

IN a small bowl, combine the reserved coconut
cream with the chilli jam, fish sauce, palm sugar
and lime juice.

JUST before serving, drain the banana blossom
and put it in a large bowl with the shredded
chicken, tomato halves, and mint and coriander
leaves. Add the dressing and gently toss to
combine the ingredients. Garnish with the
shredded makrut lime leaf.

Remove the outer leaves of the
banana blossom until you come
to the pale centre.

# CRAB AND GREEN MANGO SALAD

2 tablespoons fish sauce

2 tablespoons lime juice

2 teaspoons palm sugar

2 green bird's eye chillies, chopped

2 red bird's eye chillies, chopped

1 teaspoon ground dried shrimp

300 g (10 oz) fresh crab meat

30 g (⅔ cup) chopped mint leaves

20 g (⅓ cup) chopped coriander
  (cilantro) leaves

4 Asian shallots, finely sliced

1 green mango, flesh finely shredded

1 tomato, cut in half lengthways and
  thinly sliced

1 large green chilli, thinly sliced on
  an angle

SERVES 4

TO make a dressing, put the fish sauce, lime juice, palm sugar, bird's eye chillies and dried shrimp in a small bowl and stir to dissolve the sugar.

JUST before serving, put the crab meat, mint and coriander leaves, shallots, mango and tomato in a large bowl and toss gently.

POUR the dressing over the salad, then toss to combine and serve with the sliced chilli on top.

# HOT AND SOUR GRILLED FISH SALAD

HOT AND SOUR GRILLED
FISH SALAD

2 mackerel or whiting (about
  400 g/14 oz each fish), cleaned
  and gutted, with or without head,
  or firm white fish fillets

2 lemon grass stalks, white part
  only, finely sliced

2 Asian shallots, finely sliced

1 spring onion (scallion), finely sliced

2.5 cm (1 inch) piece of ginger,
  finely sliced

5 makrut (kaffir) lime leaves,
  finely sliced

20 g (1 cup) mint leaves

5 tablespoons lime juice

1 tablespoon fish sauce

4–5 bird's eye chillies, finely sliced

a few lettuce leaves

1 long red chilli, seeded and finely
  sliced, for garnish

SERVES 4

HEAT a barbecue or grill (broiler) to medium. If using a grill, line the tray with foil. Cook the fish for about 20 minutes on each side or until the fish is cooked and light brown. You can use a special fish-shaped griddle that opens out like tongs to make it easier to lift and turn on the barbecue.

USE your hands to remove the fish heads, backbone and other bones. Break all the fish, including the skin, into bite-sized chunks and put them in a bowl.

ADD the lemon grass, shallots, spring onion, ginger, makrut lime leaves, mint leaves, lime juice, fish sauce and chillies to the fish. Mix well, then taste and adjust the seasoning if necessary.

LINE a serving plate with lettuce leaves, then spoon the salad over the leaves. Sprinkle with chilli slices.

LAAP PET

# SPICY GROUND DUCK

LAAP MEANS 'GOOD FORTUNE'. THIS VERSION USING DUCK IS A SPECIALITY FROM AROUND UBON

RACHATHANI BUT YOU CAN USE MINCED CHICKEN INSTEAD OF DUCK. LAAP IS SERVED WITH RAW

VEGETABLES SUCH AS SNAKE BEANS, CABBAGE AND FIRM, CRISP LETTUCE.

Pound the dry-fried rice in a pestle and mortar until it forms a powder. Alternatively, you can use a small blender.

1 tablespoon jasmine rice
280 g (10 oz) minced (ground) duck
3 tablespoons lime juice
1 tablespoon fish sauce
2 lemon grass stalks, white part
   only, finely sliced
50 g (2 oz) Asian shallots,
   finely sliced
5 makrut (kaffir) lime leaves,
   finely sliced
5 spring onions (scallions),
   finely chopped
¼–½ teaspoon roasted chilli powder,
   according to taste
a few lettuce leaves
a few mint leaves, for garnish
raw vegetables such as snake
   beans, cut into lengths, cucumber
   slices, thin wedges of cabbage,
   halved baby tomatoes, to serve

SERVES 4

DRY-FRY the rice in a small pan over a medium heat. Shake the pan to move the rice around, for 6 to 8 minutes, or until the rice is brown. Using a pestle and mortar or a small blender, pound or blend the rice until it almost forms a powder.

IN a saucepan or wok, cook the duck with the lime juice and fish sauce over a high heat. Crumble and break the duck until the meat has separated into small pieces. Cook until light brown. Dry, then remove from the heat.

ADD the rice powder, lemon grass, shallots, makrut lime leaves, spring onions and chilli powder to the duck and stir together. Taste, then adjust the seasoning if necessary.

LINE a serving plate with lettuce leaves. Spoon the duck over the leaves, then garnish with mint leaves. Arrange the vegetables on a separate plate.

Add the mung bean vermicelli and mushrooms to the seafood, then the flavourings.

Unloading mussels in Pattaya.

YAM WUN SEN THALEH

# HOT AND SOUR VERMICELLI WITH MIXED SEAFOOD

ONE OF THE MILDER CLASSIC SALADS FOUND ALL OVER THAILAND, OFTEN MADE JUST WITH PRAWNS, BUT HERE MADE WITH SEAFOOD. THE VERMICELLI USED BECOMES ALMOST TRANSLUCENT WHEN SOAKED. AS THE DRESSING IS ABSORBED QUICKLY, DON'T MAKE THE SALAD TOO FAR AHEAD.

110 g (4 oz) mung bean vermicelli
175 g (6 oz) mixed raw medium prawns (shrimp), squid tubes and scallops
8 mussels
15 g (½ oz) dried black fungus (about half a handful)
1½ tablespoons vegetable oil
4–5 garlic cloves, finely chopped
3 tablespoons lime juice
1 tablespoon fish sauce
2 lemon grass stalks, white part only, finely sliced
3 Asian shallots, finely sliced
¼–½ teaspoon chilli powder or 2–3 bird's eye chillies, finely sliced
3 spring onions (scallions), finely chopped
a few lettuce leaves
1 long red chilli, seeded and finely sliced, for garnish

SERVES 4

SOAK the mung bean vermicelli in boiling water for 1 to 2 minutes, or until soft, then drain and roughly chop.

PEEL and devein the prawns and cut each prawn along the back so it opens like a butterfly (leave each prawn joined along the base and at the tail, leaving the tail attached).

PEEL off the skin from the squid tubes, rinse the insides and cut the tubes into 5 mm (¼ inch) rings. Remove any dark vein from the scallops.

SCRUB the mussels and remove their hairy beards. Discard any open mussels and any that don't close when tapped on the work surface.

SOAK the black fungus in boiling water for 2 to 3 minutes or until soft, then drain and roughly chop them.

HEAT the oil in a small wok or frying pan and stir the garlic over a medium heat until light brown. Transfer the fried garlic to a small bowl.

IN a saucepan or wok, cook the prawns, squid rings and mussels over a medium heat with the lime juice and fish sauce for 1 to 2 minutes or until the prawns open and turn pink. Add the scallops and cook for 1 minute. Discard any unopened mussels. Add the vermicelli and mushrooms to the pan and cook for another 2 minutes or until the vermicelli is cooked. Remove from the heat.

ADD the lemon grass, shallots, chilli powder or chillies, and spring onions and mix well. Taste, then adjust the seasoning if necessary.

LINE a serving plate with lettuce leaves, then spoon the seafood over the leaves. Sprinkle with chilli slices and the fried garlic.

## YAM NEUA YANG NAHM TOKE

# SLICED STEAK WITH HOT AND SOUR SAUCE

YAM NEUA YANG NAHM TOKE LITERALLY MEANS 'BEEF GRILLED ON BURNING HOT CHARCOAL TILL THE JUICES FALL'. THIS NORTHERN SALAD IS EATEN WITH STICKY RICE AND IS PERFECT WITH BEER, THAI WHISKY OR WINE. SERVE THE SALAD WITH RAW VEGETABLES SUCH AS GREEN CABBAGE.

Heat the barbecue to medium before adding the meat.

350 g (12 oz) lean sirloin, rump
   or fillet steak
2 tablespoons fish sauce
4 tablespoons lime juice
1 teaspoon sugar
¼ teaspoon roasted chilli powder
3–4 Asian shallots, finely sliced
a few lettuce leaves, to serve
20 g (⅓ cup) roughly chopped
   coriander (cilantro) leaves,
   for garnish
15 g (¼ cup) roughly chopped mint
   leaves, for garnish

SERVES 4

HEAT a barbecue or grill (broiler) to medium. If using a grill, line the tray with foil. Put the beef on the grill rack and sprinkle both sides with salt and pepper. Cook for 5 to 7 minutes on each side, turning occasionally. Fat should drip off the meat and the meat should cook slowly enough to remain juicy and not burn. Using a sharp knife, slice the cooked beef crossways into strips.

MIX the fish sauce, lime juice, sugar and chilli powder in a bowl. Add the Asian shallots and the slices of beef. Taste, then adjust the seasoning if necessary.

LINE a serving plate with lettuce leaves, then spoon the mixture over the leaves. Sprinkle with coriander and mint leaves.

Paddy fields in Phetchaburi.

TROPICAL FRUIT Thai fruit is sold whole, or completely prepared, usually cut into segments ready to eat. In either case the fruit is sold by weight. Jackfruit (kha-nun), (top left), have a flavour like fruit salad and a slightly rubbery texture. The tough, spiky, outer skin is peeled away to reveal segments of flesh (bottom left) which are then seeded. Rambutan (ngaw), above, have a bright red coating with soft, green spikes.

# FRUIT

A WONDERFUL ARRAY OF TROPICAL FRUIT (PHON-LA-MAI) IS TAKEN FOR GRANTED AS PART OF EVERYDAY LIFE IN THAILAND. FRUIT IS EATEN AT BREAKFAST, AS A SNACK, INSTEAD OF DESSERT, AND APPEARS IN MANY RECIPES. IT IS ALSO JUICED, DRIED, PICKLED AND SALTED. IT IS SOLD ON EVERY STREET CORNER OF EVERY CITY, TOWN AND VILLAGE.

Tropical fruit grows well throughout Thailand. A drive around the countryside reveals rows of fruit trees, and not just in orchards. Even in town, every spare scrap of land has a banana tree or two, a papaya tree and possibly a mango tree. Fresh fruit is often sold prepared. You can buy a plastic bag full of fruit pieces with a wooden skewer for picking them up. Most bags come with a little bag of seasoning. Thais like a balance of flavours and fruit is no exception. Salt, sugar and a little chilli powder perk up fruit and bring out the flavour.

Fruit is used extensively in Thai cuisine. Jackfruit, carambola (starfuit), mangosteen, green mango and lychees are all used in curries. Salads are made from green mango, papaya or pieces of pomelo. Bananas are steamed in their skins and

BANANAS *(kluay)* There are more than 20 varieties of banana in Thailand, each with individual characteristics and taste. All are used in cooking. Bananas are sold at floating markets and green bananas hang ripening from the eaves of houses. Medium *kluay naam waa* are the typical banana. Egg bananas *(kluay khai)* are referred to as 'lady fingers' elsewhere. Sugar bananas are small and sweet.

served for breakfast, or speared on skewers and roasted over hot coals to be eaten as a roadside snack. Desserts include the ubiquitous banana fritters, as well as bananas simmered in coconut milk, sticky rice with mango, macerated fruit and grilled bananas. Modern cuisine has embraced ice creams and sorbets made in every imaginable fruit flavour.

## FRUIT DRINKS

Fresh fruit juices *(naam pan)* often come as something of a shock to the visitor to Thailand. Just as fresh fruit is eaten with a special seasoning of chilli, sugar and salt, fruit juices are 'seasoned' with salt. Juices are usually chopped fruit, water and ice whizzed in a blender with a pinch of salt. Most vendors have a couple of blenders on the go at once.

CARVED FRUIT is one of the main forms of table decoration in smart hotels and restaurants in Thailand. Large fruit such as papaya, pomelo and melons are carved into intricate open flower patterns and smaller fruit or half fruit are carved into smaller flowers. Leaves are carved out of pieces of skin and the whole lot arranged in sumptuous displays. One melon takes an experienced carver just 20 minutes to complete.

## PRESERVED FRUIT (phon-la-mai chaei im)

In Thailand, as many types of fruit as possible are preserved by dry-salting, pickling, candying or drying. Bags of preserved fruit are sold at stalls and are as common as bags of sweets in the West.

## DURIAN

The infamous durian (thurian) is the most anticipated fruit in the Thai calendar. Although 'tasting like heaven but smelling like hell', durian has a reputation second to none. The putrid smell lingers but is not enough to deter enthusiasts from loving the rich pulp. Different varieties are available throughout the year but, when not in season, a desire for it can be satisfied by products such as freeze-dried chips or deep-fried slices.

## FRUIT SEASONS

Bananas, guavas, jackfruit, limes, watermelons, oranges, papayas, pomelos and pineapples are always present. European fruit is now grown in cooler uplands, especially in the hill area north-west and north of Chiang Mai. Orchards of peaches, cherries and apples, as well as hothouses with strawberries growing, are seen alongside lychees.

March sees the arrival of mangoes, followed by mangosteens in April and lychees in May. The following five months are the best time for fruit: custard apples, longans, rambutans, rose apples, sapodilla, carambola, jujube, langsat, santol and sala come into season and then go again. The colder winter months are the time for year-round and non-indigenous fruit.

**CUSTARD APPLE** *(nauy naa)*
Also known as sugar apple, these have a sweet flavour and a soft creamy texture. They have hard black seeds.

**DRAGON FRUIT** *(keow mang korn)* An extraordinary bright fruit, pink and green on the outside, these have a crisp, sweet, watery white flesh and tiny black seeds.

**GUAVA** *(farang)* Guava have a perfumed flesh that is astringent when unripe. Pink- or white-fleshed, they will overpower other fruit when ripe.

**MANGOSTEEN** *(mang-khut)*
These have a hard casing and a soft, white, sweet flesh that comes in segments. There are about two seeds per fruit.

**DURIAN** *(thurian)* Banned from airlines, hotel rooms and public places, durian inspires love or hate. Without its rotten smell the sweet flesh would be better liked.

**CARAMBOLA** *(ma feuang)*
Also known as starfruit because of their cross-sectional appearance. Eaten with both savoury and sweet dishes.

**GREEN MANGO** *(mamuang)*
Used in savoury dishes for their souring properties. Shredded into salads *(yam)* or added to curries and soups.

**SAPODILLA** *(lamut)* Soft fruit with a fuzzy yellow-brown skin. Each has three or four flat black seeds. The flesh browns and sweetens as it ripens.

**ROSE APPLE** *(chom-phuu)*
Crisp fruit eaten more for their texture than flavour. Often served with dips like *naam phrik* and alongside savoury food.

**LONGKONG** These grow in clusters like a bunch of grapes. The skins cover segments of translucent white flesh and green seeds.

**POMELO** *(som-oh)* Giant citrus fruit with a sweet juicy flesh. Eaten out of the hand or sometimes broken into segments and used in salads *(yam)*.

**MAKRUT LIME** *(luk ma-krut)*
Also kaffir limes, these knobbly limes are used for their zest rather than for their bitter juice. Peel off the zest in sections.

FISH & SHELLFISH

Whether you are using chillies or capsicums, remove all the seeds and membrane.

Fishing in Phang-nga.

# CURRIED FISH STEAMED IN BANANA CHILLIES

A SMOOTH CURRIED CUSTARD WITH FISH FILLS THESE CHILLIES. CHOOSE A SELECTION OF COLOURS FOR A VERY STRIKING DISH. RED, YELLOW AND ORANGE CHILLIES KEEP THEIR COLOUR BETTER THAN GREEN ONES. YOU CAN ALSO USE SMALL CAPSICUMS OF VARIOUS COLOURS.

FISH FILLING
4–5 dried long red chillies
3 garlic cloves, roughly chopped
1–2 Asian shallots, roughly chopped
4 coriander (cilantro) roots,
    roughly chopped
1 lemon grass stalk, white part only,
    finely sliced
1 cm (½ inch) piece of galangal,
    finely chopped
1 teaspoon makrut (kaffir) lime zest
    or 2 makrut (kaffir) lime leaves,
    finely sliced
1 teaspoon shrimp paste
¼ teaspoon salt
275 g (10 oz) firm white fish fillets,
    cut into 1 cm (½ inch) pieces,
    or small raw prawns (shrimp)
    or small scallops
400 ml (1⅔ cups) coconut milk
    (page 279)
2 eggs
2 tablespoons fish sauce

10 banana chillies,
    or small capsicums (peppers),
    preferably elongated ones
2 handfuls of Thai sweet basil
    leaves
2 tablespoons coconut cream
3–4 makrut (kaffir) lime leaves,
    finely sliced, for garnish
1 long red chilli, seeded, finely
    sliced, for garnish

SERVES 4

TO MAKE the fish filling, using a pestle and mortar or blender, pound or blend the chillies, garlic, shallots and coriander roots together. Add the lemon grass, galangal, makrut lime zest, shrimp paste and salt, one ingredient at a time, until the mixture forms a curry paste.

IN a bowl, combine the curry paste, fish, coconut milk, eggs and fish sauce. Keep stirring in the same direction for 10 minutes, then cover and refrigerate for 30 minutes to set slightly.

IF USING chillies, or if the capsicums are the long ones, make a long cut with a sharp knife, or if they are the round ones, cut a small round slice from the tops. Remove the seeds and membrane, then clean the chillies or capsicums and pat them dry. Place a few basil leaves in the bottom of each. Spoon in the fish mixture until it nearly reaches the top edge.

FILL a wok or a steamer pan with water, cover and bring to a rolling boil over a high heat. Place the chillies or capsicums on a plate. Use a plate that will fit on the rack of a traditional bamboo steamer basket or on a steamer rack inside the wok or pan. Taking care not to burn your hands, set the basket or rack over the water and put the plate on the rack. Reduce the heat to a simmer. Cover and cook for 15 to 20 minutes. Check and replenish the water after 10 minutes.

TURN off the heat and transfer the chillies or capsicums to a serving plate. Spoon the coconut cream on top and sprinkle with makrut lime leaves and sliced chilli.

# FISH STEAMED IN BANANA LEAF

THE DELICIOUS AROMATIC CURRIED FISH CUSTARD FILLING FOR THIS DISH IS THE SAME ONE AS ON THE PRECEDING PAGE. IN THIS RECIPE THE FISH CUSTARD IS STEAMED IN INDIVIDUAL BANANA LEAF CUPS AND THIS RESULTS IN A DELIGHTFUL EXOTIC PRESENTATION.

banana leaves
2 handfuls of Thai sweet basil
   leaves
fish filling (page 104)
2 tablespoons coconut cream
3–4 makrut (kaffir) lime leaves,
   finely sliced
1 long red chilli, seeded and finely
   sliced, for garnish

MAKES 6 banana cups

TO SOFTEN the banana leaves and prevent them splitting, put them in a hot oven for about 10 to 20 seconds, or blanch them briefly. Cut the leaves into 12 circles 15 cm (6 inches) in diameter with the fibre running lengthways. Place one piece with the fibre running lengthways and another on top with the fibre running across. Make a 1 cm (½ inch) deep tuck 4 cm (1½ inches) long (4 cm in from the edge and no further) and pin securely with a small sharp toothpick. Repeat at the opposite point and at the two side points, making four tucks altogether. Flatten the base as best you can. Repeat to make 6 square-shaped cups. Place a few basil leaves in the bottom of each cup and spoon in fish filling until three-quarters full.

FILL a wok or a steamer pan with water, cover and bring to a boil over a high heat. Place the banana cups on a plate. Use a plate that will fit on the rack of a traditional bamboo steamer basket or on a steamer rack inside the wok or pan. (If your wok or pan has a special steaming plate that will hold the cups flat, you may not need to put them on a separate plate.) Taking care not to burn your hands, set the rack or basket over the water and put the plate on the rack. Reduce the heat to a simmer. Cover and cook for 15 to 20 minutes. Check and replenish the water after 10 minutes.

WHEN the cups are cooked the filling will puff and rise slightly. Turn off the heat and carefully transfer the cups to a serving plate. Spoon a little coconut cream on top and sprinkle with lime leaves and sliced chilli.

Use a bowl or plate as a guide when cutting the banana leaves. Pin together with toothpicks.

Cut the crab into quarters, leaving the legs attached. Add the coconut milk mixture and onion after 5 minutes.

Snack seller in Bangkok.

# CRACKED CRAB WITH CURRY POWDER

THIS CRAB RECIPE IS ONE OF THE FEW THAI DISHES TO USE CURRY POWDER AS A MAIN FLAVOURING. BOUGHT CURRY POWDER (LOOK FOR A THAI BRAND) IS USUALLY VERY GOOD AND THIS IS WHAT THAI COOKS WOULD USE BUT THERE IS A RECIPE ON PAGE 287 IF YOU NEED TO MAKE YOUR OWN.

1 live crab, 500 g (1 lb 2 oz)
170 ml (⅔ cup) coconut milk
  (page 279)
1 tablespoon light soy sauce
½ tablespoon oyster sauce
2 teaspoons Thai curry powder
  (page 287) or bought Thai
  curry powder
¼ teaspoon sugar
2 tablespoons vegetable oil
3–4 garlic cloves, finely chopped
1 small onion, cut into 3 wedges
2 spring onions (scallions),
  finely sliced
½ long red chilli, seeded and
  finely sliced, for garnish
a few coriander (cilantro) leaves,
  for garnish

SERVES 4

PUT the crabs in the freezer for 1 hour. Leaving the legs attached, cut the crab in half through the centre of the shell from head to rear. Cut in half again from left to right (quartering the crab), with legs attached to each quarter. Twist off and remove the upper shell pieces. Discard the stomach sac and the soft gill tissue. Using crackers or the back of a heavy knife, crack the crab claws to make them easier to eat. If the claws are too big, cut them in half.

MIX the coconut milk, light soy sauce, oyster sauce, curry powder and sugar in a bowl.

HEAT the oil in a wok or frying pan. Stir-fry the garlic over a medium heat until light brown. Add the crab and stir-fry for about 4 to 5 minutes. Add the coconut mixture and onion and continue stir-frying for another 5 to 7 minutes or until the crab meat is cooked through and the sauce is reduced and very thick. Add the spring onions. Taste, then adjust the seasoning if necessary. Spoon onto a serving plate and sprinkle with sliced chilli and coriander leaves.

NEUNG HAWY LAI KRA-CHAI

# CLAMS AND MUSSELS WITH CHINESE KEYS

450 g (1 lb) mixed clams and
    mussels in the shell
75 g (3 oz) Chinese keys,
    finely sliced
2.5 cm (1 inch) piece of galangal,
    cut into 7–8 slices
1 long red chilli, seeded and
    finely chopped
2 teaspoons fish sauce
½ teaspoon sugar
a few sprigs of basil leaves,
    for garnish

SERVES 2

SCRUB the clams and mussels and remove any hairy beards from the mussels. Discard any open mussels or clams and any that don't close when tapped on the work surface. Wash them all in several changes of cold water until the water is clear, then put them in a large bowl, cover with cold water and soak for 30 minutes. This helps remove the sand from the clams.

PUT the clams and mussels, Chinese keys, galangal and chopped chilli in a large saucepan or wok. Cover loosely and cook over a medium heat for 5 minutes, shaking the pan frequently. Add the fish sauce and sugar and toss together. Discard any unopened shells. Serve the clams and mussels in a large bowl. Garnish with basil leaves.

PHAT HAWY MALAENG PHUU TA-KHRAI

# MUSSELS WITH LEMON GRASS

450 g (1 lb) mussels or clams
    in the shell
1½ tablespoons vegetable oil
2–3 garlic cloves, finely chopped
1 small onion, finely chopped
3 lemon grass stalks, white part
    only, finely sliced
2.5 cm (1 inch) piece of galangal,
    cut into 7–8 slices
2 long red chillies, seeded and
    finely chopped
1 tablespoon fish sauce
1 tablespoon lime juice
½ teaspoon sugar
25 g (1 cup) holy basil leaves,
    roughly chopped

SERVES 2

SCRUB the mussels or clams and remove any hairy beards from the mussels. Discard any open mussels or clams and any that don't close when tapped on the work surface. If using clams, wash them in several changes of cold water until the water is clear, then put them in a large bowl, cover with cold water and soak for 30 minutes. This helps remove the sand from the clams.

HEAT the oil in a wok and stir-fry the garlic, onion, lemon grass, galangal and chillies over a medium heat for 1 to 2 minutes or until fragrant.

ADD the mussels or clams and stir-fry for a few minutes. Add the fish sauce, lime juice and sugar. Cover loosely and cook over a medium heat for 5 to 7 minutes, shaking the wok frequently. Cook until the shells are open, discarding any unopened shells. Mix in the chopped holy basil. Taste, then adjust the seasoning if necessary.

SERVE the steamed mussels or clams hot in a large bowl.

MUSSELS WITH LEMON
GRASS

# DEEP-FRIED FISH WITH SWEET AND SOUR SAUCE

WHEN SERVING WHOLE FISH, LIFT OFF PORTIONS FROM THE TOP FILLETS AND THEN REMOVE THE BONES IN ONE PIECE SO YOU CAN ACCESS THE FILLETS UNDERNEATH. THE FLAVOUR OF SWEET AND SOUR SAUCE WORKS EXTREMELY WELL WITH ALL TYPES OF FISH.

400 g (14 oz) St Peters fish, sea bream, red snapper or grey mullet
3½ tablespoons plain (all-purpose) flour
pinch of ground white pepper
vegetable oil, for deep-frying
225 g (8 oz) tin pineapple slices in juice, each slice cut into 4 pieces (reserve the juice)
1½ tablespoons plum sauce or ketchup
2½ teaspoons fish sauce
1 tablespoon sugar
1½ tablespoons vegetable oil
3–4 garlic cloves, finely chopped
1 medium onion, cut into 8 slices
½ red capsicum (pepper), cut into bite-sized pieces
1 small cucumber (skin left on), cut into bite-sized pieces
1 medium tomato, cut into 8 wedges, or 4 baby tomatoes
a few coriander (cilantro) leaves, for garnish

SERVES 2

CLEAN and gut the fish, leaving the head on. Thoroughly dry the fish and score it three or four times on both sides with a sharp knife. Rub the fish inside and out with a pinch of salt. Put 3 tablespoons of the flour and the pepper on a plate and press the fish lightly into it until coated with flour from head to tail. Shake off any excess.

HEAT 10 cm (4 inches) oil in a large wok or pan big enough to deep-fry the whole fish. Drop a small cube of bread into the oil and if it sizzles straight away, the oil is ready. Lower the heat to medium and gently slide the fish into the oil. Be careful as the hot oil may splash. Deep-fry the fish on just one side (but make sure the oil covers the whole fish) for about 15 to 20 minutes or until the fish is cooked and light brown (if you cook the fish until it is very brown, the fish will be too dry). Drain, then put on paper towels before transferring to a warm plate. Keep warm.

MEANWHILE, mix all the pineapple juice (about 6 tablespoons) with the remaining flour, plum sauce or ketchup, fish sauce and sugar in a small bowl until smooth.

REMOVE the oil from the wok or pan and heat 1½ tablespoons clean oil in the same wok or pan. Stir-fry the garlic over a medium heat for 1 minute or until light brown. Add the onion and capsicum and stir-fry for 1 to 2 minutes. Add the pineapple, cucumber, tomato and pineapple juice mixture. Stir together for another minute. Taste, then adjust the seasoning if necessary. Pour all over the warm fish and garnish with a few coriander leaves.

PLAA NEUNG GEAM BOUI

# STEAMED FISH WITH PRESERVED PLUM

BUY AN APPROPRIATELY LARGE STEAMER FOR THIS RECIPE OR USE THE STEAMER RACK OF YOUR WOK. BOTH WILL WORK EQUALLY WELL. PRESERVED PLUMS ARE SOLD IN JARS IN ASIAN SUPERMARKETS AND, ONCE OPENED, THEY WILL KEEP IN THE REFRIGERATOR FOR SOME TIME.

1 tablespoon light soy sauce
½ teaspoon sugar
1 large or 2 smaller pomfret, flounder, or turbot, (total weight about 1 kg/2 lb 4 oz)
50 g (2 oz) mushrooms, roughly sliced
2 small preserved plums, bruised
5 cm (2 inch) piece of ginger, julienned
4 spring onions (scallions), sliced diagonally
2 long red or green chillies, seeded and finely sliced
a few coriander (cilantro) leaves, for garnish
a sprinkle of ground white pepper

SERVES 4

IN a small bowl, mix the light soy sauce and sugar.

CLEAN and gut the fish, leaving the head/s on. Dry the fish thoroughly. Score the fish three or four times on both sides with a sharp knife. Place the fish on a deep plate slightly larger than the fish itself. Use a plate that will fit on the rack of a traditional bamboo steamer basket or on a steamer rack inside the wok. Sprinkle the mushrooms, preserved plums and ginger over the fish. Pour the light soy sauce mixture all over the fish.

FILL a wok or a steamer pan with water, cover and bring to a rolling boil over a high heat. Taking care not to burn your hands, set the rack or basket over the boiling water and put the plate with the fish on the rack. Reduce the heat to a simmer. Cover and steam for 25 to 30 minutes (depending on the variety and size of the fish) or until the skewer will slide easily into the fish. Check and replenish the water every 10 minutes or so. Remove the fish from the steamer. Serve on the same plate. Sprinkle with spring onions, chillies, coriander leaves and pepper.

Deep-fry the basil leaves in two batches until they are crispy.

Pattaya market.

PLA THAWT BAI HOHRAPHAA

# DEEP-FRIED FISH WITH CHILLIES AND BASIL

THIS IS ONE OF THE MOST POPULAR FISH DISHES IN THAILAND AND YOU CAN USE MOST TYPES OF FISH TO MAKE IT. THE FISH HAS A MILDLY SPICY FLAVOUR AND IS GARNISHED WITH DEEP-FRIED CHILLI AND BASIL LEAVES. THE DUSTING OF FLOUR ISN'T TRADITIONAL BUT IT HELPS CRISP THE SKIN.

1 large or 2 smaller red snapper
  (total weight about 1 kg/2 lb 4 oz)
3 tablespoons plain (all-purpose)
  flour
pinch of ground black pepper
1½ tablespoons vegetable oil
½ tablespoon red curry paste
  (page 276) or bought paste
2 tablespoons palm sugar
2 tablespoons fish sauce
vegetable oil, for deep-frying
a handful of Thai sweet basil leaves
1 dried long red chilli, cut into
  5 mm (¼ inch) pieces,
  seeds discarded
3 makrut (kaffir) lime leaves,
  very finely sliced, for garnish

SERVES 4

CLEAN and gut the fish, leaving the head/s on. Thoroughly dry the fish. Score the fish three or four times on both sides with a sharp knife. Rub the fish inside and out with a pinch of salt. Place the flour and ground pepper on a plate and press the fish lightly into it until coated with flour from head to tail. Shake off any excess.

HEAT the oil in a small saucepan, add the red curry paste and stir over a medium heat for 1 to 2 minutes or until fragrant. Add the sugar, fish sauce and 2 tablespoons water and cook for another 1 to 2 minutes or until the sugar has dissolved. Remove from the heat.

HEAT 10 cm (4 inches) oil in a large wok or pan big enough to deep-fry the whole fish. When the oil is hot, drop a few basil leaves into it. If they sizzle immediately, the oil is ready. Deep-fry half of the basil leaves for 1 minute or until they are all crispy. Remove with a slotted spoon and drain on paper towels. Deep-fry the rest.

IN the same wok, deep-fry the dried chilli pieces for a few seconds over a medium heat until light brown. Be careful not to burn them. Remove with a slotted spoon and drain on paper towels. Lower the heat to medium and gently slide the fish into the oil. Be careful as the hot oil may splash. Deep-fry the fish on just one side (but make sure the oil covers the whole fish) for about 5 to 10 minutes or until the fish is cooked and light brown (if you cook the fish until it is very brown, it will be too dry). Drain off the oil and drain the fish on paper towels.

PUT the curry sauce in the wok and gently warm it. Add the fish and coat both sides with the sauce. Transfer the fish to a warm plate with any remaining sauce and sprinkle with crispy basil, fried chilli pieces and the makrut lime leaves.

PLAA PHAO

# GRILLED FISH WITH GARLIC AND CORIANDER

BANANA LEAVES ARE USED IN THIS RECIPE TO PROTECT THE FISH FROM DIRECT HEAT AS WELL AS TO
ADD A SUBTLE EXTRA FLAVOUR. THE LEAVES WILL CHAR AS THEY COOK. YOU WILL FIND BANANA
LEAVES IN ASIAN SUPERMARKETS, OFTEN IN THE FREEZER CABINETS.

4 red tilapa, grey/red mullet, or
  mackerel (about 300 g/
  10 oz each)
8–10 garlic cloves, roughly chopped
6 coriander (cilantro) roots, chopped
1 teaspoon ground white pepper
1 teaspoon salt
1 tablespoon vegetable oil
8 pieces of banana leaf
a chilli sauce, to serve

SERVES 4

CLEAN and gut the fish, leaving the heads on. Dry
the fish thoroughly. Score each fish three or four
times on both sides with a sharp knife.

USING a pestle and mortar or a small blender,
pound or blend the garlic, coriander roots,
ground pepper, salt and oil into a paste. Rub the
garlic paste inside the cavities and all over each
fish. Cover and marinate in the refrigerator for at
least 30 minutes.

TO SOFTEN the banana leaves and prevent
them from splitting, put them in a hot oven for
10 to 20 seconds, or blanch them briefly. Using
two pieces of banana leaf, each with the grain
running at right angles to the other, wrap each fish
like a parcel. Pin the ends of the banana leaves
together with toothpicks.

HEAT a grill (broiler) or barbecue to medium.
Barbecue or grill (broil) the fish for about
15 minutes on each side or until the fish is light
brown and cooked. To make the fish easier to lift
and turn during cooking, you can place the fish in
a fish-shaped griddle that opens out like tongs.
Transfer the fish to a serving plate. Serve with a
chilli sauce.

Score the fish, then prepare it
and wrap in the banana leaves.

Cut the ginger into thin slices before cutting it into matchsticks.

# DEEP-FRIED FISH WITH GINGER

ALTHOUGH THAI FISH ARE NOT TRADITIONALLY COATED IN FLOUR BEFORE BEING FRIED, IT WILL HELP GIVE A CRISPER SKIN. MAKE SURE THE FISH IS REALLY WELL COOKED AND CRISP OR THE SAUCE WILL MAKE IT SOGGY. IF YOU CAN'T GET ONE LARGE FISH, USE SEVERAL SMALLER ONES INSTEAD.

15 g (½ oz) dried black fungus (about half a handful)
1 large or 2 smaller red snapper, grey mullet, sea bass or grouper (total weight about 1 kg/2 lb 4 oz)
3 tablespoons plain (all-purpose) flour
pinch of ground black pepper
1 tablespoon oyster sauce
1 tablespoon light soy sauce
¼ teaspoon sugar
vegetable oil, for deep-frying
1½ tablespoons vegetable oil
4 garlic cloves, roughly chopped
1 small carrot, cut into matchsticks
2 cm (¾ inch) piece of ginger, cut into matchsticks
2 spring onions (scallions), finely sliced, for garnish

SERVES 4

SOAK the black fungus in hot water for 2 to 3 minutes until soft, then drain the fungus and finely chop.

CLEAN and gut the fish, leaving the head/s on. Dry the fish thoroughly. Score the fish three or four times on both sides with a sharp knife. Rub the fish inside and out with a pinch of salt. Put the flour and ground pepper on a plate and lightly press the fish into it until it is coated all over. Shake off any excess flour.

MIX the oyster sauce, light soy sauce, sugar and 2 tablespoons water in a small bowl.

HEAT 10 cm (4 inches) oil in a large wok or saucepan big enough to deep-fry the whole fish. When the oil seems hot, drop a small piece of spring onion into the oil. If it sizzles straight away, the oil is ready. Lower the heat to medium and gently slide the fish into the oil. Be careful as the hot oil may splash. Deep-fry the fish on just one side (but make sure the oil covers the whole fish) for about 5 to 10 minutes or until the fish is cooked and light brown (if you cook the fish until it is very brown, the fish will be too dry). Drain on paper towels before transferring to a warm plate. Keep warm. Drain off the oil.

HEAT 1½ tablespoons clean oil in the same wok and stir-fry the garlic over a medium heat until light brown. Add the carrot, ginger, mushrooms and the sauce mixture and stir-fry for 1 to 2 minutes. Taste, then adjust the seasoning if necessary. Pour over the warm fish and sprinkle with spring onions.

Dried fish on sale.

PLAA THAWT SAHM ROT

# DEEP-FRIED FISH WITH THREE-FLAVOURED SAUCE

YOU CAN USE LIME JUICE IN THIS DISH IF YOU PREFER A CLEAR SAUCE, OR TAMARIND FOR A THICK OR DARKER-COLOURED SAUCE. USE TWO OR FOUR SMALLER FISH IF YOU CAN'T FIND ONE FISH LARGE ENOUGH. GARNISH WITH HOLY BASIL IF YOU CAN FIND IT.

1 x 350 g (12 oz) sea bream, red snapper or grey mullet
3 tablespoons plain (all-purpose) flour
pinch of ground black pepper
vegetable oil, for deep-frying
4–5 garlic cloves, roughly chopped
5 long red chillies, seeded and roughly chopped
4–5 Asian shallots, roughly chopped
3 coriander (cilantro) roots, finely chopped
3 tablespoons palm sugar
2 tablespoons fish sauce
3 tablespoon tamarind purée or lime juice
a few holy basil or Thai sweet basil leaves, for garnish

SERVES 2

CLEAN and gut the fish, leaving the head on. Dry the fish thoroughly. Score the fish three or four times on both sides with a sharp knife.

RUB the fish inside and out with a pinch of salt. Put the flour and ground pepper on a plate or dish and press the fish lightly into it until coated with flour from head to tail. Shake off any excess.

HEAT 10 cm (4 inches) oil in a large wok or pan big enough to deep-fry the whole fish. When the oil seems hot, drop a piece of shallot into the oil. If it sizzles straight away, the oil is ready. Lower the heat to medium and gently slide the fish into the oil. Be careful as the hot oil may splash. Deep-fry the fish on just one side (but make sure the oil covers the whole fish) for about 15 to 20 minutes or until the fish is cooked and light brown (if you cook the fish until it is brown, it will be too dry). Drain, then put on paper towels before transferring to a warm plate. Keep warm.

WHILE the fish is cooking, use a pestle and mortar or a small blender to pound or blend the garlic, chillies, shallots and coriander roots together into a rough paste.

HEAT 1 tablespoon oil in a wok or frying pan and stir-fry the chilli paste over a medium heat for 2 to 3 minutes or until fragrant. Add the palm sugar, fish sauce and tamarind purée or lime juice, and cook for 2 to 3 minutes or until the sugar has dissolved. Pour the warm chilli sauce over the fish and garnish with basil leaves.

Deep-fry the whole floured fish on one side only, making sure the oil covers the fish.

Selling vegetables at the floating market.

FISH Fish caught locally tend to be sold locally, unless caught commercially. The fish market at Ranong deals both in fish caught locally and those found further out to sea. At smaller markets, fresh fish is sold just caught, or even still alive, from buckets and tanks. Market vendors kill and clean the fish as it is sold. Most fish are cooked with the head still on and the cheeks of the fish are considered to be the tastiest parts.

# FISH & SEAFOOD

FRESHWATER FISH AND SEAFOOD ARE AN INTEGRAL PART OF THE THAI DIET. AS A FOOD THEY ARE SECOND ONLY TO RICE IN IMPORTANCE. WHILE FRESH SEAFOOD IS EATEN BY MOST PEOPLE ON AN ALMOST DAILY BASIS, FISH SAUCE AND SHRIMP PASTE ARE ALSO PART OF THE THAI LEXICON OF FLAVOURINGS USED IN VIRTUALLY EVERY DISH.

Fish and seafood are caught all over Thailand, along the 2710 kilometres (1685 miles) of coastline, from lakes, inland waterways, ponds and even in amongst rice paddies and in puddles left after storms. Fishing is done by commercial boats, communities and individuals. Wholesale markets at every major port send the catch both abroad and to markets throughout Thailand. Inland, fish is likely to be local freshwater fish, sold at markets with only a tiny amount on offer.

Different areas have particular specialities and marine-based industries. People make their own fish sauce, but commercial operations can be found on the Gulf of Thailand. The Isthmus of Kra and islands are famous for fresh fish and shellfish, grilled (broiled) or barbecued, and Pattaya for crayfish.

Whole cooked fish like these mackerel (top left) can also be bought from most markets. Prawns and shrimp are very popular: tiger prawns (right) are farmed on a large scale and are particularly meaty. Small shrimp are dried and are either ground to a powder or soaked in a liquid before use. Good-quality dried prawns have a deep orange colour, as shown here.

Inland, during April and May, giant catfish are fished from the Mekong in the North. Prawns are farmed in mangroves, though often not to the benefit of the environment or locals.

## PRESERVED, DRIED AND FERMENTED SEAFOOD

The majority of what comes out of Thailand's water is dried, preserved or converted to shrimp paste and fish sauce. The sun is used to dry fish, shrimp and squid all along the coast, spread out on mats or on bamboo frames (right). Fish, crabs and shellfish such as mussels are also pickled. Small amounts of preserved or dried fish add lots of flavour and can be used to dress rice or vegetables. Shrimp paste forms the base of dips eaten with fresh vegetables. Dried roast squid, a street snack, is the equivalent of a bag of chips.

## FISH SAUCE FACTORY

**MAKING FISH SAUCE** The Tang Sang Hah factory makes several brands of fish sauce for home and overseas markets. Originally made in ceramic jars (left), fish sauce is now made in concrete tanks. Anchovies are brought to the factory from all over Thailand and mixed with salt before being put into tanks. Each tank is two metres (six feet, six inches) deep and the factory has three thousand tanks. New fish supplies come in every day but the fish shown above (centre) is one month old and has already started to break down. The tanks are covered and the

fish ferments in its own juices, aided by the heat of the sun and preserved by the salt. The fish and juices are mixed as they sit in the tanks and when the fish has fermented for 12 months it has broken down enough for the solids to sink to the bottom of the tank, leaving the fish sauce at the top. The liquid is drawn off from the tanks, then filtered and blended and tested for quality. A small amount of sugar is added to each batch but nothing else. It is then bottled. Fish sauce is sold in different grades and the type of bottle reflects how good it is. Second-

grade fish sauce that is slightly saltier is bottled in larger plastic bottles and, according to the firm, is very popular with noodle vendors who use large amounts of it on a daily basis. Third-grade sauce is also sold in larger plastic bottles. Twelve-month-old premium grade sauce with a good fishy flavour is sold as Tiparos brand and it comes in small glass bottles with gold labels and has a red, blue and white logo (centre right and right). First-grade sauce with a yellow label (left) is the next best.

CRABS *(puu)* Crab meat is popular in fried rice dishes and with noodles. Whole crab are often chopped into pieces and fried with curry powder.

SQUID *(plaa meuk kluay)* Squid is eaten both fresh and dried. Fresh squid is usually blanched in boiling water, rather than being fried, to keep it tender.

POMFRET *(plaa-ja-la-met)* This is a good eating fish found all over Asia. Pomfret are particularly good when fried whole and also in curries.

RAY These are caught further off the coast and are not a common fish in Thailand, though they may be found in areas where there is a large fish market.

PRAWNS *(kung)* Tiger prawns are popular in soups, curries and noodle dishes. A prawn (shrimp) dish will be on every Thai menu.

CARP *(plaa tapian)* A favourite in South-East Asia and China, carp are freshwater fish found in local inland markets. Farmed and wild.

TILAPIA *(plaa nin)* Freshwater fish are often farmed, sometimes on a small scale in backyards or ponds. Usually steamed or fried.

CLAMS *(hawy lai)* Clams, eaten in soups and curries, are treated much like oysters with which they share a generic name — *hawy*.

## PRESERVED FISH

Salted, dried and pickled fish and seafood are common. As well as keeping efficiently, preserved fish and seafood deliver more flavour. Dried shrimp, often ground, are common. Many varieties are available (far left). Pickled mussels (centre left) are used in stir-fries and salads. Semi-dried fish (centre right) are used in curries, or deep-fried and used in salads. Tiny dried fish (right) are deep-fried and crumbled into dishes.

MEAT & GAME

The pork is threaded onto skewers using a sewing action.

Selling souvenirs in Mae Tang.

MUU PING

# PORK ON STICKS

JUST LIKE SATAY, PORK ON STICKS IS A POPULAR SNACK AS WELL AS MAKING AN EXCELLENT PARTY
FOOD AND IS IDEAL FOR INFORMAL OCCASIONS SUCH AS BARBECUES. IT CAN BE SERVED WITH RICE
OR STICKY RICE. NO ADDITIONAL SAUCE IS NECESSARY WITH THIS RECIPE.

1 kg (2 lb 4 oz) fillet of pork
250 ml (1 cup) coconut milk
  (page 279)
2 tablespoons coconut sugar
2 tablespoons light soy sauce
2 tablespoons oyster sauce
110 g (4 oz) Asian shallots,
  roughly chopped
4 garlic cloves, roughly chopped
5 coriander (cilantro) roots,
  finely chopped
2.5 cm (1 inch) piece of ginger,
  sliced
1½ teaspoons ground turmeric
¼ teaspoon ground white pepper
25 bamboo skewers, 18–20 cm
  (7–8 inches) long

MAKES 25

CUT the pork into pieces 4 cm (1½ inches) wide
x 8 cm (3 inches) long x 5 mm (¼ inch) thick and
put them in a bowl.

MIX the coconut milk, sugar, light soy sauce,
oyster sauce, shallots, garlic, coriander roots,
ginger, turmeric and pepper in a bowl until the
sugar has dissolved. Pour over the meat and mix
using your fingers or a spoon. Cover with plastic
wrap and refrigerate for at least 5 hours, or
overnight, turning occasionally.

SOAK the bamboo skewers in water for 1 hour to
help prevent them from burning during cooking.

THREAD a piece of the marinated pork onto each
skewer as if you were sewing a piece of material.
If some pieces are small, thread two pieces onto
each stick. Heat a barbecue or grill (broiler) to high
heat. If using a grill, line the grill tray with foil.

BARBECUE for 5 to 7 minutes on each side, or
grill (broil) the pork for 10 minutes on each side,
until cooked through and slightly charred. Turn
frequently and brush the marinade sauce over the
meat during the cooking. If using the grill, cook a
good distance below the heat. Serve hot or warm.

## MUU YANG
# BARBECUED PORK SPARE RIBS

2–3 garlic cloves, chopped

1 tablespoon chopped coriander (cilantro) roots or ground coriander

6 tablespoons palm sugar

7 tablespoons plum sauce or tomato ketchup

2 tablespoons light soy sauce

2 tablespoons oyster sauce

1 teaspoon ground pepper

½ teaspoon ground star anise (optional)

900 g (2 lb) pork spare ribs, chopped into 13–15 cm (5–6 inch) long pieces (baby back, if possible — ask your butcher to prepare it)

SERVES 4

USING a pestle and mortar or a small blender, pound or blend the garlic and coriander roots into a paste. In a large bowl, combine all the ingredients and rub the marinade all over the ribs with your fingers. Cover with plastic wrap and marinate in the refrigerator for at least 3 hours, or overnight.

PREHEAT the oven to 180°C/350°F/Gas 4 or heat a barbecue or grill (broiler). If cooking in the oven, place the ribs with all the marinade in a baking dish. Bake for 45 to 60 minutes, basting several times during cooking. If barbecuing, put the ribs on the grill, cover and cook for 45 minutes, turning and basting a couple of times. If the ribs do not go sufficiently brown, grill (broil) them for 5 minutes on each side until well browned and slightly charred. If using a grill, line the grill tray with foil. Cook the pork, turning several times and brushing frequently with the remaining sauce, until the meat is cooked through and slightly charred.

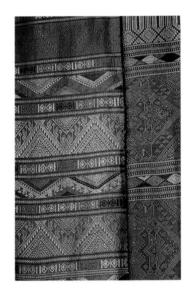

## MUU THAWT
# DEEP-FRIED PORK SPARE RIBS

5 coriander (cilantro) roots, chopped

3 garlic cloves, finely chopped

1 tablespoon fish sauce

1½ tablespoons oyster sauce

½ teaspoon ground white pepper

900 g (2 lb) pork spare ribs, chopped into 4–5 cm (1½–2 inch) long pieces (baby back, if possible—ask your butcher to prepare it)

vegetable oil, for deep-frying

sweet chilli sauce (page 284), to serve

SERVES 4

USING a pestle and mortar or a small blender, pound or blend the coriander roots and garlic into a paste. In a large bowl, combine the coriander paste, fish sauce, oyster sauce and ground pepper. Rub the marinade into the pork ribs using your fingertips, then cover and marinate in the refrigerator for at least 3 hours, or overnight.

HEAT 6 cm (2½ inches) oil in a wok or deep frying pan over a medium heat. When the oil seems hot, drop a small piece of garlic into it. If it sizzles immediately, the oil is ready. It is important not to have the oil too hot or the spare ribs will burn. Deep-fry half the spare ribs at a time for 15 to 20 minutes or until golden brown and cooked. Drain on paper towels. Serve with sweet chilli sauce.

DEEP-FRIED PORK SPARE RIBS

# DEEP-FRIED QUAIL

QUAIL WORKS WELL FOR DISHES THAT WOULD PROBABLY TRADITIONALLY HAVE USED PIGEON OR TURTLE DOVE. CHICKEN PIECES CAN ALSO BE USED BUT THE QUAILS LOOK MORE ATTRACTIVE ON THE PLATE. SERVE ALONGSIDE VEGETABLE DISHES OR USE AS A STARTER.

5 white peppercorns
5 coriander seeds
¼ teaspoon cumin seeds
1 star anise
2 garlic cloves
2 tablespoons soy sauce
½ teaspoon palm sugar
4 quails
oil, for deep-frying
roasted chilli sauce (page 283) or
    sweet chilli sauce (page 284),
    to serve

SERVES 4

USING a pestle and mortar, pound together the peppercorns, coriander seeds, cumin seeds, star anise and a pinch of salt. Add the garlic, soy sauce and palm sugar and pound to a paste.

RUB the paste all over the quails, cover and marinate in the refrigerator for at least 3 hours.

HEAT the oil in a wok until a piece of bread dropped into it sizzles and turns brown. Pat the quails dry with paper towels. Add the quails and fry them for about 10 minutes, turning them so that they cook on all sides. Make sure the oil gets inside the quails as well.

DRAIN well and sprinkle with a little more salt. Cut into quarters and serve with roasted chilli sauce or sweet chilli sauce.

Cover the quails with the paste, then marinate them. Remove the cooked quail from the oil with a slotted spoon.

MUU WAAN
# CARAMEL PORK

CARAMEL PORK HAS A RELATIVELY SWEET FLAVOUR AND IS BEST SERVED WITH STEAMED JASMINE

RICE OR STICKY RICE AND A SHARP-FLAVOURED DISH LIKE GREEN PAPAYA SALAD OR POMELO SALAD.

CARAMEL PORK WILL KEEP FOR A FEW DAYS IN THE REFRIGERATOR AND CAN BE MADE IN ADVANCE.

vegetable oil, for deep-frying
75 g (3 oz) Asian shallots, finely
    sliced
6 garlic cloves, finely chopped
500 g (1 lb 2 oz) shoulder or leg
    of pork, cut into thin slices
1 tablespoon oyster sauce
1 tablespoon light soy sauce
1 tablespoon fish sauce
4 tablespoons palm sugar
¼ teaspoon ground white pepper

SERVES 4

HEAT 5 cm (2 inches) oil in a deep saucepan or wok over a medium heat and deep-fry the shallots until they are golden brown. Be careful not to burn them. Remove them from the wok with a slotted spoon and drain on paper towels.

DRAIN the oil from the saucepan or wok, leaving 2 tablespoons in the pan. Stir-fry the garlic in the oil until light brown, then add the pork and stir-fry for a few minutes. Add the oyster sauce, light soy sauce, fish sauce, sugar and ground pepper and continue cooking for about 5 minutes, or until all the liquid has evaporated and the mixture forms a thick sticky sauce.

SPOON onto a serving plate and sprinkle with the crispy shallots. Serve as required.

Palm sugar on sale.

MUU PARLOW
# BRAISED PORK

1 large pork hock or 2 small ones
oil, for deep-frying
2 coriander (cilantro) roots, chopped
4 garlic cloves, crushed
2 teaspoons ground white pepper
4 slices of ginger
2 star anise
1 cinnamon stick
2 tablespoons palm sugar
2 tablespoons fish sauce
2 tablespoons ketchap manis
1.5 litres (6 cups) chicken stock
4 hard-boiled eggs, shells removed

SERVES 4

PUT the pork hock in a saucepan of salted water and bring to the boil. Drain and repeat, then pat dry with paper towels. Heat a wok one-quarter filled with oil until the oil is very hot. Carefully add the dried pork hock to the wok and fry on all sides until brown. Loosely cover the wok with a lid if the oil spits too much. Remove the hock and drain away all but a tablespoon of the oil.

FRY the coriander roots, garlic and pepper briefly, then add the ginger, star anise and cinnamon stick and fry for a minute. Add the palm sugar, fish sauce, ketchap manis and stock and bring to a boil. Add the hock and cook for 2 hours or until the hock meat starts to fall off the bone. Add the eggs and cook for 10 minutes. Season with salt and serve with jasmine rice.

BRAISED PORK

DRIED BEEF

## NEUA HAENG
# DRIED BEEF

coriander (cilantro) roots from
  1 bunch, finely chopped
1 teaspoon cumin seeds, roasted
2 teaspoons coriander seeds,
  roasted
4 garlic cloves
1 teaspoon white peppercorns
2 tablespoons palm sugar
2 tablespoons soy sauce
350 g (12 oz) rump steak,
  thinly sliced
oil, for deep-frying
sticky rice (page 280), to serve
a chilli sauce, to serve

SERVES 6

USING a pestle and mortar, pound together the coriander roots, cumin seeds, coriander seeds, garlic, peppercorns and a pinch of salt into a paste. Add the palm sugar and soy sauce and mix until the sugar dissolves. Add the steak and mix. Cover and marinate in the refrigerator overnight.

PREHEAT the oven to its lowest setting. Take the steak strips out of the marinade and drape them over wire cooling racks. Dry the steak strips in the oven for about 4 hours. They should be dry and leathery when they are ready.

IF THE beef is not crisp, heat some oil for deep-frying in a wok. Drop a small piece of steak into the oil and if it sizzles immediately, the oil is ready. Deep-fry the steak in batches until crisp, then drain on paper towels. Serve with sticky rice and chilli sauce.

## KAI YAANG
# GRILLED CHICKEN

IN THAILAND, THESE WHOLE GRILLED CHICKEN ARE SEEN BY THE ROADSIDE ROTATING ON OPEN SPITS. THAI CHICKENS ARE LEANER THAN THOSE FOUND IN WESTERN COUNTRIES BUT THE TASTE WILL BE SIMILAR. THERE ARE MANY FLAVOURING VARIATIONS USED FOR GRILLED CHICKENS.

MARINADE
4 coriander (cilantro) roots,
  finely chopped
4 garlic cloves, finely chopped
1 lemon grass stalk, white part only,
  finely chopped
3 tablespoons fish sauce
¼ teaspoon ground white pepper
1 teaspoon palm sugar

1 chicken, spatchcocked
sweet chilli sauce (page 284),
  to serve
lime wedges, to serve

SERVES 4

USING a pestle and mortar, pound the marinade ingredients together, then spoon into a bowl. Add the chicken and rub the marinade all over the chicken skin. Cover and marinate in the refrigerator for at least 3 hours, or overnight.

HEAT a barbecue, char-grill or grill (broiler) until very hot. Cook the chicken for 20 to 30 minutes, turning it over at regular intervals.

CUT the chicken into pieces and serve with sweet chilli sauce and lime wedges.

Chickens spit-roasted by the roadside.

CURRIES

The fruit is added towards the end of cooking.

# SNAPPER WITH GREEN BANANA AND MANGO

GREEN BANANA IS VERY STARCHY, MUCH MORE LIKE A VEGETABLE THAN A FRUIT. HERE IT USED IN A YELLOW CURRY ALONGSIDE ANOTHER FRUIT, GREEN MANGO, WHICH ACTS AS A SOURING AGENT. RAW VEGETABLES ARE OFTEN SERVED AS AN ACCOMPANIMENT TO COUNTERACT THE CHILLI HEAT.

1 teaspoon salt
1 teaspoon ground turmeric
1 small green banana or plantain,
   thinly sliced
60 ml (¼ cup) coconut cream
   (page 279)
2 tablespoons yellow curry paste
   (page 275) or bought paste
1 tablespoon fish sauce
1 teaspoon palm sugar
400 g (14 oz) snapper or other
   white fish fillets, cut into
   large cubes
315 ml (1¼ cups) coconut milk
   (page 279)
1 small green mango, cut into
   thin slices
1 large green chilli, finely sliced
12 Thai sweet basil leaves

SERVES 4

BRING a small saucepan of water to the boil. Add the salt, turmeric and banana slices and simmer for 10 minutes, then drain.

PUT the coconut cream in a wok or saucepan and simmer over a medium heat for about 5 minutes, or until the cream separates and a layer of oil forms on the surface. Stir the cream if it starts to brown around the edges. Add the curry paste, stir well to combine and cook until fragrant. Add the fish sauce and sugar and cook for another 2 minutes or until the mixture begins to darken.

ADD the fish pieces and stir well to coat the fish in the curry mixture. Slowly add the coconut milk until it has all been incorporated.

ADD the banana, mango, green chilli and most of the basil leaves to the pan and gently stir to combine all the ingredients, cooking for a minute or two. Garnish with the remaining basil.

Green mangoes.

# PRAWNS WITH THAI SWEET BASIL LEAVES

THE SAUCE FOR THIS DISH SHOULD BE THICK, HOT AND SWEET SO MAKE SURE YOUR WOK IS HOT
ENOUGH TO REDUCE THE COCONUT MILK AS IT HITS THE SURFACE.

600 g (1 lb 5 oz) raw prawns
   (shrimp)
2 tablespoons vegetable oil
2 tablespoons dry curry paste
   (page 272) or bought paste
185 ml (¾ cup) coconut milk
   (page 279)
2 teaspoons fish sauce
2 teaspoons palm sugar
a handful of Thai sweet basil leaves,
   for garnish
1 long red chilli, seeded and finely
   sliced, for garnish

SERVES 4

PEEL and devein the prawns and cut each prawn
along the back so it opens like a butterfly (leave
each prawn joined along the base and at the tail,
leaving the tail attached).

HEAT the oil in a saucepan or wok and stir-fry the
dry curry paste over a medium heat for 2 minutes
or until fragrant.

ADD the coconut milk, fish sauce and palm sugar
and cook for a few seconds. Add the prawns and
cook for a few minutes or until the prawns are
cooked through. Taste, then adjust the seasoning
if necessary. Spoon into a serving bowl and
garnish with basil leaves and chillies.

# PRAWN AND PINEAPPLE CURRY

PRAWN AND PINEAPPLE
CURRY

SPICE PASTE
4 bird's eye chillies, seeded
6 Asian shallots
2 lemon grass stalks, white part
   only, finely chopped
½ teaspoon shrimp paste
½ teaspoon ground turmeric

2 tablespoons oil
185 ml (¾ cup) coconut milk
   (page 279)
300 g (10 oz) fresh pineapple,
   cut into small wedges
2 tablespoons tamarind purée
3 makrut (kaffir) lime leaves
250 g (9 oz) raw prawns (shrimp),
   peeled and deveined
2 teaspoons fish sauce
1 tablespoon palm sugar

SERVES 4

PUT all the spice paste ingredients in a pestle and
mortar and pound to a paste. Alternatively, use a
food processor and add 2 tablespoons water.
Blend until well combined.

HEAT the oil in a wok or saucepan. Add the spice
paste and fry until fragrant. Stir in the coconut milk
and cook for 2 minutes. Add the pineapple
wedges, tamarind purée and makrut lime leaves
and simmer for 5 minutes, or until the pineapple
begins to soften.

ADD the prawns and stir well to cover them in the
sauce. Simmer for 5 to 6 minutes until the prawns
are cooked through. Stir in the fish sauce and
sugar before serving.

As soon as the curry paste is fragrant, stir in the pork, Asian shallots, ginger and peanuts.

Songathews and tuk tuks in Chiang Mai.

KAENG HANGLEH MUU

# CHIANG MAI PORK CURRY

THIS BURMESE-STYLE CURRY IS TYPICAL OF THE CHIANG MAI AREA. UNLIKE FRAGRANT THAI CURRIES, THIS HAS A SPICIER, ALMOST INDIAN FLAVOUR. NEARLY ALWAYS MADE WITH PORK, YOU WILL OCCASIONALLY FIND IT MADE WITH CHICKEN. THIS CURRY IMPROVES IF MADE IN ADVANCE.

500 g (1 lb 2 oz) pork belly,
   cut into cubes
2 tablespoons oil
2 garlic cloves, crushed
2 tablespoons Chiang Mai curry
   paste (page 272) or bought paste
4 Asian shallots, smashed with the
   blade of a cleaver
4 cm (1½ inch) piece of ginger,
   shredded
4 tablespoons roasted unsalted
   peanuts
3 tablespoons tamarind purée
2 tablespoons fish sauce
2 tablespoons palm sugar

SERVES 4

BLANCH the pork cubes in boiling water for 1 minute, then drain well.

HEAT the oil in a wok or saucepan and fry the garlic for 1 minute. Add the curry paste and stir-fry until fragrant. Add the pork, shallots, ginger and peanuts and stir briefly. Add 500 ml (2 cups) water and the tamarind purée and bring to a boil.

ADD the fish sauce and sugar and simmer for about 1½ hours or until the pork is very tender. Add more water as the pork cooks, if necessary. The meat is ready when it is very tender.

KAENG MUU PHRIK THAI ORN

# RED PORK CURRY WITH GREEN PEPPERCORNS

PEPPERCORNS ADD A DISTINCTIVE, VERY FRESH AND SPICY, NOT TOO HOT, TASTE TO THIS DISH. YOU CAN USE PORK, AS SUGGESTED, OR FINELY SLICED CHICKEN THIGH FILLETS. COOKED BABY POTATOES AND BAMBOO SHOOTS ARE A POPULAR ADDITION TO THIS CURRY.

60 ml (¼ cup) coconut cream
  (page 279)
2 tablespoons red curry paste
  (page 276) or bought paste
3 tablespoons fish sauce
1½ tablespoons palm sugar
500 g (1 lb 2 oz) lean pork,
  finely sliced
440 ml (1¾ cups) coconut milk
  (page 279)
280 g (10 oz) Thai eggplants
  (aubergines), cut in halves
  or quarters, or 1 eggplant
  (aubergine), cubed
75 g (3 oz) fresh green
  peppercorns, cleaned
7 makrut (kaffir) lime leaves,
  torn in half
2 long red chillies, seeded
  and finely sliced, for garnish

SERVES 4

PUT the coconut cream in a wok or saucepan and simmer over a medium heat for about 5 minutes, or until the cream separates and a layer of oil forms on the surface. Stir the cream if it starts to brown around the edges.

ADD the curry paste, stir well to combine and cook until fragrant. Add the fish sauce and palm sugar and cook for another 2 minutes or until the mixture begins to darken. Add the pork and stir for 5 to 7 minutes.

ADD the coconut milk to the saucepan or wok and simmer over a medium heat for another 5 minutes. Add the eggplants and green peppercorns and cook for 5 minutes. Add the makrut lime leaves. Taste, then adjust the seasoning if necessary. Transfer to a serving bowl and sprinkle with the chillies.

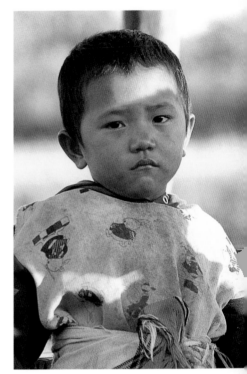

Stir-fry the curry paste to bring out the flavour before adding the rest of the ingredients.

KAENG PAA

# JUNGLE CURRY WITH PRAWNS

JUNGLE CURRY, A VERY HOT CURRY, IS COMMON TO THE COUNTRYSIDE, PARTICULARLY IN NORTHERN THAILAND. IT IS TRADITIONALLY MADE WITH LOCAL CATFISH BUT WORKS WELL WITH ANY FISH, OR WITH PRAWNS AS IN THIS RECIPE. IT CAN BE MADE WITH PORK AND MOST FRESH VEGETABLES.

JUNGLE CURRY PASTE
8 bird's eye chillies, chopped
2 cm (¾ inch) piece of galangal, chopped
2 lemon grass stalks, white part only, finely chopped
4 Asian shallots, finely chopped
4 garlic cloves, finely sliced
½ teaspoon shrimp paste

400 g (14 oz) raw prawns (shrimp)
1 tablespoon oil
4 baby sweet corn, each cut into half lengthways on an angle
75 g (3 oz) Thai eggplants (aubergines), cut in halves or quarters
50 g (2 oz) pea eggplants (aubergines)
50 g (2 oz) straw or button mushrooms, halved if large
1 tablespoon fish sauce
½ teaspoon palm sugar
2–3 makrut (kaffir) lime leaves, torn into pieces, for garnish
a handful of holy basil or Thai sweet basil leaves, for garnish

SERVES 4

PUT all the jungle curry paste ingredients in a pestle and mortar and pound until smooth. Alternatively, put them in a food processor with 2 tablespoons water and process to a smooth paste.

PEEL and devein the prawns and cut each prawn along the back so it opens like a butterfly (leave each prawn joined along the base and at the tail).

HEAT the oil in a wok or saucepan and stir-fry 2 tablespoons of the curry paste until fragrant. Add 410 ml (1⅔ cups) water and reduce the heat to medium. Add the sweet corn and eggplants and cook for 1 to 2 minutes. Add the mushrooms and prawns, fish sauce and sugar. Cook until the prawns open and turn pink. Taste, then adjust the seasoning if necessary. Sprinkle with the makrut lime leaves and basil leaves before serving.

KAENG MATSAMAN NEUA

# MASSAMAN CURRY WITH BEEF

THIS CURRY HAS MANY CHARACTERISTICS OF SOUTHERN THAI COOKING. THE SWEET FLAVOURS AND
SPICES DOMINATE, EVEN THOUGH THE CURRY IS MODERATELY HOT. IT ALSO HAS A SOUR TASTE FROM
THE TAMARIND. THIS DISH IS ONE OF THE FEW THAI DISHES WITH POTATOES AND PEANUTS.

2 pieces of cinnamon stick
10 cardamom seeds
5 cloves
2 tablespoons vegetable oil
2 tablespoons massaman curry
    paste (page 276) or bought paste
800 g (1 lb 12 oz) beef flank or
    rump steak, cut into 5 cm (2 inch)
    cubes
410 ml (1⅔ cups) coconut milk
    (page 279)
250 ml (1 cup) beef stock
2–3 potatoes, cut into 2.5 cm
    (1 inch) pieces
2 cm (¾ inch) piece of ginger,
    shredded
3 tablespoons fish sauce
3 tablespoons palm sugar
110 g (⅔ cup) ready-made roasted
    salted peanuts, without skin
3 tablespoons tamarind purée

SERVES 4

DRY-FRY the cinnamon stick, cardamom seeds
and cloves in a saucepan or wok over a low heat.
Stir all the ingredients around for 2 to 3 minutes or
until fragrant. Remove from the pan.

HEAT the oil in the same saucepan or wok and
stir-fry the massaman paste over a medium heat
for 2 minutes or until fragrant.

ADD the beef to the pan and stir for 5 minutes.
Add the coconut milk, stock, potatoes, ginger, fish
sauce, palm sugar, three-quarters of the roasted
peanuts, tamarind purée and the dry-fried spices.
Reduce the heat to low and gently simmer for
50 to 60 minutes until the meat is tender and the
potatoes are just cooked. Taste, then adjust the
seasoning if necessary. Spoon into a serving bowl
and garnish with the rest of the roasted peanuts.

Floating vendor.

As with many Thai curries, this one cooks relatively quickly. Keep the meat moving around the wok until you add the liquid.

# PANAENG BEEF CURRY

PANAENG CURRY IS A DRY, RICH, THICK CURRY MADE WITH SMALL AMOUNTS OF COCONUT MILK AND A DRY (PANAENG) CURRY PASTE, WHICH HAS RED CHILLIES, LEMON GRASS, GALANGAL AND PEANUTS. IT IS NOT TOO HOT AND HAS A SWEET AND SOUR TASTE. YOU CAN USE ANY TENDER CUT OF BEEF.

2 tablespoons vegetable oil
2 tablespoons dry curry paste
  (page 272) or bought paste
700 g (1 lb 9 oz) beef flank steak,
  sliced into strips
185 ml (¾ cup) coconut milk
  (page 279)
1 tablespoon fish sauce
1 tablespoon palm sugar
3 tablespoons tamarind purée
2 makrut (kaffir) lime leaves, finely
  sliced, for garnish
½ long red chilli, seeded and finely
  sliced, for garnish
cucumber relish (page 287),
  to serve

SERVES 4

HEAT the oil in a saucepan or wok and stir-fry the curry paste over a medium heat for 2 minutes or until fragrant.

ADD the beef and stir for 5 minutes. Add nearly all of the coconut milk, the fish sauce, palm sugar and tamarind purée and reduce to a low heat. Simmer, uncovered, for 5 to 7 minutes. Although this is meant to be a dry curry, you can add a little more water during cooking if you feel it is drying out too much. Taste, then adjust the seasoning if necessary.

SPOON the curry into a serving bowl, spoon the last bit of coconut milk over the top and sprinkle with makrut lime leaves and chilli slices. Serve with cucumber relish.

Busy bustling Bangkok.

KAENG KHIAW-WAAN KAI

# GREEN CURRY WITH CHICKEN

THIS FAMILIAR CLASSIC, WHICH SHOULD NEVER BE EXTREMELY HOT, HAS AS ITS BASE A PASTE OF CHILLIES, GALANGAL AND LEMON GRASS. BITTER VEGETABLES SUCH AS THAI EGGPLANT OFFSET THE SWEETNESS OF THE COCONUT CREAM. TENDER STEAK CAN BE USED INSTEAD OF CHICKEN.

60 ml (¼ cup) coconut cream
(page 279)
2 tablespoons green curry paste
(page 275) or bought paste
350 g (12 oz) skinless chicken thigh
fillets, sliced
440 ml (1¾ cups) coconut milk
(page 279)
2½ tablespoons fish sauce
1 tablespoon palm sugar
350 g (12 oz) mixed Thai eggplants
(aubergines), cut into quarters,
and pea eggplants (aubergines)
50 g (2 oz) galangal, julienned
7 makrut (kaffir) lime leaves,
torn in half
a handful of Thai sweet basil leaves,
for garnish
1 long red chilli, seeded and finely
sliced, for garnish

SERVES 4

PUT the coconut cream in a wok or saucepan and simmer over a medium heat for about 5 minutes, or until the cream separates and a layer of oil forms on the surface. Stir the cream if it starts to brown around the edges. Add the curry paste, stir well to combine and cook until fragrant.

ADD the chicken and stir for a few minutes. Add nearly all of the coconut milk, the fish sauce and palm sugar and simmer over a medium heat for another 5 minutes.

ADD the eggplants and cook, stirring occasionally, for about 5 minutes or until the eggplants are cooked. Add the galangal and makrut lime leaves. Taste, then adjust the seasoning if necessary. Spoon into a serving bowl and sprinkle with the last bit of coconut milk, as well as the basil leaves and chilli slices.

Various types of eggplant are used in Thailand and the bitter taste is very popular. They don't take long to cook.

Shrimp paste on sale.

KAENG KARII KAI

# YELLOW CHICKEN CURRY WITH PEPPERCORNS

FRESH PEPPERCORNS HAVE A FRAGRANT, PUNGENT QUALITY THAT LIFTS THE FLAVOUR OF ANY CURRY IN WHICH THEY ARE USED. YOU SHOULD BEWARE OF EATING A WHOLE SPRIG IN ONE GO THOUGH AS, JUST LIKE THE PEPPER THEY BECOME, THEY ARE EXTREMELY HOT.

60 ml (¼ cup) coconut cream
  (page 279)
2 tablespoons yellow curry paste
  (page 275) or bought paste
1 tablespoon fish sauce
2 teaspoons palm sugar
¼ teaspoon turmeric
600 g (1 lb 5 oz) chicken thigh
  fillets, cut into thin slices
440 ml (1¾ cups) coconut milk
  (page 279)
100 g (3 oz) bamboo shoots,
  thinly sliced
4 sprigs fresh green peppercorns
4–6 makrut (kaffir) lime leaves
12 Thai sweet basil leaves

SERVES 4

PUT the coconut cream in a wok or saucepan and simmer over a medium heat for about 5 minutes, or until the cream separates and a layer of oil forms on the surface. Stir the cream if it starts to brown around the edges.

ADD the curry paste, stir well to combine and cook until fragrant. Add the fish sauce, palm sugar and turmeric and stir well. Cook for 2 to 3 minutes, stirring occasionally, until the mixture darkens.

ADD the chicken to the pan and stir to coat all the pieces evenly in the spice mixture. Cook over a medium heat for 5 minutes, stirring occasionally and adding the coconut milk a tablespoon at a time to incorporate. Add the bamboo shoots, peppercorns, lime and basil leaves and cook for another 5 minutes.

KAENG PHET PLA KUP NAW MAI

# RED CURRY WITH FISH AND BAMBOO SHOOTS

ALTHOUGH THERE ARE MANY STYLES IN THE LARGE RANGE OF THAI RED CURRIES, ALL HAVE THE DEFINING CHARACTERISTIC RED COLOUR. RED CURRIES ARE QUITE LIQUID COMPARED TO DRY CURRIES SUCH AS PANAENG. BE SURE TO USE A FIRM FISH THAT WON'T FALL APART.

60 ml (¼ cup) coconut cream
   (page 279)
2 tablespoons red curry paste
   (page 276) or bought paste
440 ml (1¾ cups) coconut milk
   (page 279)
1½–2 tablespoons palm sugar
3 tablespoons fish sauce
350 g (12 oz) skinless firm white
   fish fillets, cut into 3 cm (1¼ inch)
   cubes
275 g (10 oz) tin bamboo shoots
   in water, drained, cut
   into matchsticks
50 g (2 oz) galangal, finely sliced
5 makrut (kaffir) lime leaves,
   torn in half
a handful of Thai sweet basil leaves,
   for garnish
1 long red chilli, seeded and finely
   sliced, for garnish

SERVES 4

PUT the coconut cream in a wok or saucepan and simmer over a medium heat for about 5 minutes, or until the cream separates and a layer of oil forms on the surface. Stir the cream if it starts to brown around the edges. Add the curry paste, stir well to combine and cook until fragrant.

STIR in the coconut milk, then add the sugar and fish sauce and cook for 2 to 3 minutes. Add the fish and bamboo shoots and simmer for about 5 minutes, stirring occasionally, until the fish is cooked.

ADD the galangal and makrut lime leaves. Taste, then adjust the seasoning if necessary. Spoon onto a serving plate and sprinkle with the basil leaves and sliced chilli.

The fish should be cut into bite-sized pieces and the bamboo shoots into matchsticks.

This curry, with its combination of coconut milk, duck and fruit, is very rich. Cook the lychees for only a few minutes.

KAENG PHET PET YAANG

# RED CURRY WITH ROASTED DUCK AND LYCHEES

IN THAILAND, THIS SPECIALITY DISH IS OFTEN SERVED DURING THE TRADITIONAL FAMILY FEASTING THAT ACCOMPANIES CELEBRATIONS INCLUDING THE ORDINATION OF BUDDHIST MONKS, WEDDINGS AND NEW YEAR. THIS IS VERY RICH, SO SERVE IT ALONGSIDE A SALAD TO CUT THROUGH THE SAUCE.

60 ml (¼ cup) coconut cream (page 279)
2 tablespoons red curry paste (page 276) or bought paste
½ roasted duck, boned and chopped
440 ml (1¾ cups) coconut milk (page 279)
2 tablespoons fish sauce
1 tablespoon palm sugar
225 g (8 oz) tin lychees, drained
110 g (4 oz) baby tomatoes
7 makrut (kaffir) lime leaves, torn in half
a handful of Thai sweet basil leaves, for garnish
1 long red chilli, seeded and finely sliced, for garnish

SERVES 4

PUT the coconut cream in a wok or saucepan and simmer over a medium heat for about 5 minutes, or until the cream separates and a layer of oil forms on the surface. Stir the cream if it starts to brown around the edges. Add the curry paste, stir well to combine and cook until fragrant.

ADD the roasted duck and stir for 5 minutes. Add the coconut milk, fish sauce and palm sugar and simmer over a medium heat for another 5 minutes. Add the lychees and baby tomatoes and cook for 1 to 2 minutes. Add the makrut lime leaves. Taste, then adjust the seasoning if necessary. Spoon into a serving bowl and sprinkle with the basil leaves and sliced chilli.

KAENG KUNG MANGKAWN
# SPICY LOBSTER AND PINEAPPLE CURRY

EVEN THOUGH THIS RED CURRY IS EXPENSIVE BECAUSE OF THE LOBSTER, IT IS EXCELLENT FOR SPECIAL OCCASIONS. YOU CAN USE LARGE PRAWNS OR CRAB HALVES IF YOU LIKE. ALSO, YOU CAN MAKE THE SAUCE AND SERVE IT WITH BARBECUED LOBSTER HALVES.

When the mixture has darkened, stir in the pineapple pieces.

60 ml (¼ cup) coconut cream
(page 279)
2 tablespoons red curry paste
(page 276) or bought paste
1 tablespoon fish sauce
1 tablespoon palm sugar
250 ml (1 cup) coconut milk
(page 279)
200 g (7 oz) fresh pineapple,
cut into bite-sized wedges
300 g (10 oz) lobster tail meat
3 makrut (kaffir) lime leaves,
2 roughly torn and 1 shredded
1 tablespoon tamarind purée
50 g (1 cup) Thai sweet basil
leaves, for garnish
1 large red chilli, finely sliced,
for garnish

SERVES 4

PUT the coconut cream in a wok or saucepan and simmer over a medium heat for about 5 minutes, or until the cream separates and a layer of oil forms on the surface. Stir the cream if it starts to brown around the edges.

ADD the curry paste, stir well to combine and cook until fragrant. Add the fish sauce and sugar and stir to combine. Cook for 4 to 5 minutes, stirring constantly. The mixture should darken.

STIR in the coconut milk and the pineapple. Simmer for 6 to 8 minutes to soften the pineapple. Add the lobster tail meat, makrut lime leaves, tamarind purée and basil leaves. Cook for another 5 to 6 minutes until the lobster is firm. Serve with basil leaves and sliced chilli on top.

Beaches in Khao Sok National Park.

Use wet hands to roll the fish mixture into balls. Drop them all into the curry at the same time so they cook evenly.

# GREEN CURRY WITH FISH BALLS

THIS IS A CLASSIC DISH USING FISH BALLS OR DUMPLINGS RATHER THAN PIECES OF FISH BUT, IF TIME IS SHORT, SLICES OF FISH ARE PERFECTLY ACCEPTABLE. THE FISH IS PROCESSED, THEN POUNDED, TO GIVE IT MORE TEXTURE. SERVE WITH SALTED EGGS, PAGE 287, AND RICE.

350 g (12 oz) white fish fillets, without skin and bone, roughly cut into pieces

60 ml (¼ cup) coconut cream (page 279)

2 tablespoons green curry paste (page 275) or bought paste

440 ml (1¾ cups) coconut milk (page 279)

350 g (12 oz) mixed Thai eggplants (aubergines), quartered, and pea eggplants (aubergines)

2 tablespoons fish sauce

2 tablespoons palm sugar

50 g (2 oz) galangal, finely sliced

3 makrut (kaffir) lime leaves, torn in half

a handful of holy basil leaves, for garnish

½ long red chilli, seeded and finely sliced, for garnish

SERVES 4

IN a food processor or a blender, chop the fish fillets into a smooth paste. (If you have a pestle and mortar, pound the fish paste for another 10 minutes to give it a chewy texture.)

PUT the coconut cream in a wok or saucepan and simmer over a medium heat for about 5 minutes, or until the cream separates and a layer of oil forms on the surface. Stir the cream if it starts to brown around the edges. Add the curry paste, stir well to combine and cook until fragrant. Add nearly all of the coconut milk and mix well.

USE a spoon or your wet hands to shape the fish paste into small balls or discs, about 2 cm (¾ inch) across, and drop them into the coconut milk. Add the eggplants, fish sauce and sugar and cook for 12 to 15 minutes, stirring occasionally, until the fish and eggplants are cooked.

STIR in the galangal and makrut lime leaves. Taste, then adjust the seasoning if necessary. Spoon into a serving bowl and sprinkle with the last bit of coconut milk, basil leaves and sliced chilli.

CURRY PASTES (khreuang kaeng) are made at home using a granite pestle and mortar. Dry-roasted coriander seeds, black pepper and cumin make up a base. These are finely ground together first. Next, the fresh ingredients are prepared, here by Sompon Nabnian: whole green 'sky-pointing' chillies, chopped galangal, sliced fresh turmeric, sliced lemon grass stalks and Thai sweet basil leaves (stalks removed).

# FLAVOURINGS

THAI CUISINE IS BUILT ON A LARGE NUMBER OF HIGHLY FLAVOURED AROMATIC INGREDIENTS. THESE ARE USED, DESPITE THEIR DIVERSITY, TO PRODUCE AN OVERALL EFFECT OF SOME SOPHISTICATION, BALANCE AND SUBTLTY.

Though curry pastes often include dry spices, the majority of Thai seasonings are fresh and pungent. These define the flavour that is 'Thai', as well as being responsible for adding texture to dishes. Thai flavourings are used to give as harmonious effect as possible, the balance of hot, sour, sweet and salty being paramount. Also important is fragrance.

HOT (phed) Heat, in nearly all cases, comes from chillies, though it is sometimes supplemented with fresh green peppercorns or black or white pepper. There are about a dozen chillies used in Thai cuisine, each type with a different aroma, flavour, and degree of heat (see page 174). Chillies are used fresh or dried, depending on the recipe.

SOUR (priaw) Sour comes from lime juice, the zest and leaves of makrut (kaffir) limes, tamarind, and to a lesser extent, ambarella (a South-East Asian fruit like a small mango). Sour can also come from coconut vinegar or pickles.

SWEET (waan) Sweetness is imparted by the use of palm sugar, coconut sugar, cane sugar and coconut milk.

SALTY (khem) Fish sauce and shrimp paste add saltiness to a dish. Salt itself is used as an ingredient but never as a condiment, except when sprinkled on fresh fruit.

COMMERCIAL CURRY PASTES These pastes, shown here at the Valcom factory, are made in the same way a homemade paste would be, except on a larger scale. Fresh ingredients such as garlic, shallots, galangal, chillies and lemon grass are peeled and then washed. These are then mixed with spices and herbs in a large bin before being fed into a large mincer. The paste is minced two or three times, depending on

The fresh ingredients are put into a pestle and mortar along with some shrimp paste, coriander (cilantro) root, garlic, makrut (kaffir) lime zest and tamarind, then pounded for about 15 minutes until the paste is smooth. Handmade curry pastes have a more intense flavour than those made by machine because the ingredients are crushed rather than chopped. A heavy Thai granite pestle and mortar makes pounding easier.

## FRAGRANCE

The aroma of various herbs, vegetables, rhizomes and leaves add a unique quality to Thai dishes. Robust herbs and roots such as lemon grass, ginger, galangal, turmeric, Chinese keys and coriander (cilantro) roots are used to make pastes and can be cooked for a reasonable length of time. Garlic and shallots are also important and they are often simply smashed with the blade of a cleaver rather then being peeled and finely chopped. Leaf herbs such as coriander (cilantro), Thai sweet basil, lemon and holy basil, and common mint occur frequently. Less well known herbs include long-leaf coriander *(phak chii)*. These are at their most aromatic when eaten raw, or cooked for the bare minimum of time. Sprigs of fresh herbs such as mint *(sa-ra-nae)* and Thai sweet basil *(bai horapha)* are also eaten alongside some dishes. Fragrant pandanus leaves are used as a wrapping and as a flavouring. They are said to have a vanilla flavour, and green pandanus essence is used much like vanilla essence in many sweets.

the label it is to be sold under, and it gets finer each time. The paste is then heated to pasteurize it before being put into sterilized bottles and labelled. Commercial curry pastes such as this are mainly sold abroad though some of them are used within Thailand, especially as supermarket, rather than market, shopping becomes more popular. Valcom make red, green, massaman and tom yam pastes.

CHILLIES *(phrik)* Up to a dozen types of chilli appear in Thai cuisine despite the fact that the plant is not indigenous to the area. Chillies add both colour and flavour to dishes. From left to right, bottom row: red chillies *(phrik chinda)*, named after their growing area; green and red 'bird's eye' or 'mouse dropping' *(phrik khii nuu)* chillies, the hottest chilli available in Thailand; 'sky-pointing' chillies *(phrik chii faa)*, green and red, are used both fresh and dried; orange chillies *(phrik leuang)*, rare outside Thailand, have a hot and sour flavour.

**TOM YAM FLAVOURINGS**
Bundles of flavourings are sold already portioned out, each geared towards a particular dish, as here for tom yam soup.

**GALANGAL** *(khaa)* A rhizome with a hot peppery flavour. Young pale galangal can be eaten in pieces. Older redder pieces are best used in curry pastes.

**CORIANDER** *(phak chii)*
Coriander (cilantro) is sold in bunches with the root on. All parts of the plant, the roots, stalks and leaves, are used.

**TURMERIC** *(kha-min)* There are three types of turmeric, red (above), zedoary and white. The first two are used as an ingredient. White is eaten raw.

**MAKRUT LIME LEAVES**
*(bai makrut)* Makrut (kaffir) limes have double leaves and a knobbly skin. The leaves and zest are used but not the bitter juice.

**ASIAN SHALLOTS** *(hawm)*
These tiny red shallots are ubiquitous to Thai cuisine. They are often used whole, smashed with a cleaver.

**HOLY BASIL** *(bai ka-phrao)*
This basil has a hot sharp flavour and comes in both white (above) and red varieties. Used with seafood and stir-fries.

**LEMON GRASS** *(ta-khrai)*
A popular flavouring, only the tender middle of lemon grass stalks should be used. Peel down to the purple ring.

**LEMON BASIL** *(bai maeng-lak)*
The least common of the basils, this is used in soups and fish curries. It has a citrus flavour and delicate leaves.

**TAMARIND** *(ma-khaam)*
Shown here in pod form, more commonly sold as dried pulp which is fibrous. It is soaked and a tart liquid extracted before use.

**GARLIC** *(kra-tiam)*
Milder, sweeter and smaller than European garlic, Thai garlic is often fried in oil and used as a crisp garnish.

**THAI SWEET BASIL**
*(bai horapha)* Used in curries and soups, this has a very intense aniseed fragrance that is instantly recognizable as Thai.

# STIR-FRIES

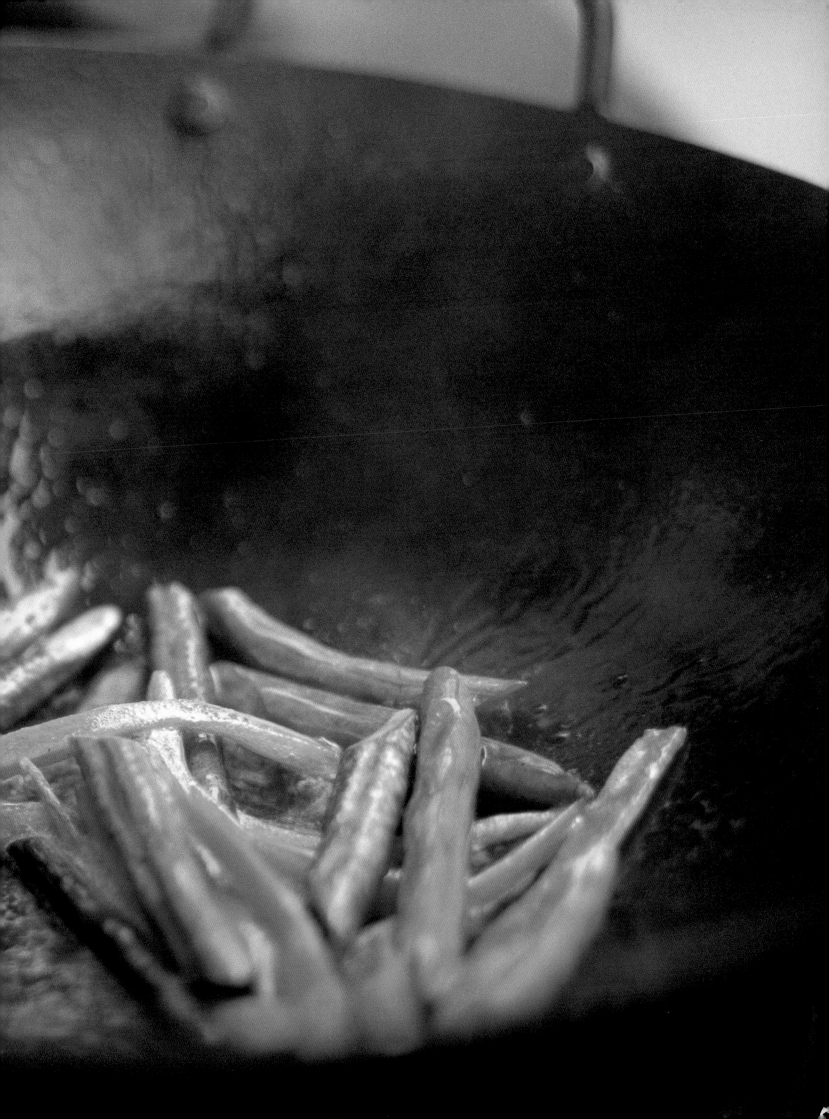

# BEEF WITH THAI SWEET BASIL LEAVES

THAI SWEET BASIL IS ONE OF THE TROPICAL HERBS WITH A DISTINCTIVE FLAVOUR AND PERFUME THAT INSTANTLY EVOKES THAI CUISINE. NO OTHER HERB WILL DO AS A SUBSTITUTE FOR THIS RECIPE. YOUR WOK SHOULD BE VERY HOT AND THE DISH SHOULD TAKE NO MORE THAN 7 OR 8 MINUTES TO COOK.

1 tablespoon fish sauce
3 tablespoons oyster sauce
4 tablespoons vegetable or
   chicken stock, or water
½ teaspoon sugar
2 tablespoons vegetable oil
4 garlic cloves, finely chopped
3 bird's eye chillies, lightly crushed
   with the side of a cleaver
500 g (1 lb 2 oz) tender rump or
   fillet steak, finely sliced
1 medium onion, cut into thin
   wedges
2 handfuls of Thai sweet basil
   leaves

SERVES 4

MIX the fish sauce, oyster sauce, stock and sugar in a small bowl.

HEAT the oil in the wok or frying pan and stir-fry half the garlic over a medium heat until light brown. Add half the crushed chillies and half the meat and stir-fry over a high heat for 2 to 3 minutes or until the meat is cooked. Remove from the wok and repeat with the remaining garlic, chillies and meat. Return all the meat to the wok.

ADD the onion and the fish sauce mixture and stir-fry for another minute.

ADD the basil leaves and stir-fry until the basil begins to wilt. Taste, then adjust the seasoning if necessary. Spoon onto a serving plate.

Warorot market.

PHAT NEUA TAO JIAW DAM

# BEEF WITH BLACK BEAN SAUCE

THIS CHINESE DISH APPEARS IN VARIOUS GUISES IN THAILAND. HERE IT IS MADE WITH SNAKE BEANS AND BEEF. BLACK BEANS ARE OFTEN CALLED FERMENTED OR PRESERVED BLACK BEANS AND ARE SOLD IN JARS OR TUBS IN SHOPS THAT SPECIALIZE IN CHINESE FOOD.

1 tablespoon black beans, rinsed
  and roughly mashed
3 tablespoons vegetable or chicken
  stock, or water
1 tablespoon fish sauce
1 tablespoon oyster sauce
1 tablespoon sesame oil
½ teaspoon sugar
1 tablespoon vegetable oil
3–4 garlic cloves, finely chopped
250 g (9 oz) tender rump or fillet
  steak, finely sliced
½ carrot, cut into fine matchsticks
4 snake beans, cut into 5 cm
  (2 inch) lengths
2 spring onions (scallions), cut into
  2.5 cm (1 inch) lengths
a few coriander (cilantro) leaves,
  for garnish

SERVES 4

Mix the black beans with the stock, sauces, oil and sugar.

MIX the black beans, stock, fish sauce, oyster sauce, sesame oil and sugar in a small bowl.

HEAT the oil in a wok or frying pan and stir-fry half the garlic over a medium heat until light brown. Add half the meat and stir-fry over a medium heat for 3 to 4 minutes or until the meat is cooked. Remove from the wok. Repeat with the remaining garlic and meat. Return all the garlic and meat to the wok.

ADD the carrot, beans and the sauce mixture to the wok and stir-fry for another 1 to 2 minutes. Taste, then adjust the seasoning if necessary. Stir in the spring onions and cook for a few seconds. Spoon onto a serving plate and garnish with coriander leaves.

Floating markets at Damnoen Saduak.

KAI PHAT BAI KA-PHRAO

# CHICKEN WITH CRISPY HOLY BASIL LEAVES

THIS IS ONE OF THE MOST COMMON DISHES YOU WILL COME ACROSS IN THAILAND. HOLY BASIL COMES IN TWO COLOURS, RED AND GREEN. IT HAS A HOT, SLIGHTLY SHARP FLAVOUR AND IS OFTEN USED IN CONJUNCTION WITH CHILLIES IN STIR-FRIES. SERVE WITH PLENTY OF RICE.

500 g (1 lb 2 oz) skinless chicken breast fillets, thinly sliced
4–5 garlic cloves, finely chopped
4–5 small red or green bird's eye chillies, lightly crushed
1 tablespoon fish sauce
2 tablespoons oyster sauce
vegetable oil, for deep-frying
2 handfuls of holy basil leaves
2 tablespoons vegetable or chicken stock, or water
½ teaspoon sugar
1 red capsicum (pepper), cut into bite-sized pieces
1 medium onion, cut into thin wedges

SERVES 4

MIX the chicken, garlic, chillies, fish sauce and oyster sauce in a bowl. Cover with plastic wrap and marinate in the refrigerator for at least 30 minutes.

HEAT 5 cm (2 inches) oil in a wok or deep frying pan over a medium heat. When the oil seems hot, drop a few basil leaves into it. If they sizzle immediately, the oil is ready. Deep-fry three-quarters of the basil leaves for 1 minute or until they are all crispy. Lift out with a slotted spoon and drain on paper towels. Discard the remaining oil.

HEAT 2 tablespoons oil in the same wok or frying pan and stir-fry half the chicken over a high heat for 3 to 4 minutes. Remove from the pan and repeat with the remaining chicken. Return all the chicken to the wok.

ADD the stock and sugar to the wok, then the capsicum and onion, and stir-fry for another 1 to 2 minutes. Stir in the fresh basil leaves. Taste, then adjust the seasoning if necessary. Garnish with the crispy basil leaves.

KAI PHAT MET MUANG HIMAPHAAN

# CHICKEN WITH CASHEW NUTS

THIS POPULAR DISH IS TYPICALLY CHINESE BUT APPEARS ON MANY THAI RESTAURANT MENUS. THE CASHEWS ARE ACTUALLY A THAI ADDITION. FRYING THE CASHEW NUTS SEPARATELY BRINGS OUT THEIR FLAVOUR AND ADDS A MORE 'NUTTY' TASTE TO THE DISH.

1–2 dried long red chillies
1 tablespoon fish sauce
2 tablespoons oyster sauce
3 tablespoons chicken or vegetable
  stock, or water
½–1 teaspoon sugar
4 tablespoons vegetable oil
80 g (½ cup) cashew nuts
4–5 garlic cloves, finely chopped
500 g (1 lb 2 oz) skinless chicken
  breast fillets, finely sliced
½ red capsicum (pepper), cut into
  thin strips
½ carrot, sliced diagonally
1 small onion, cut into 6 wedges
2 spring onions (scallions), cut into
  1 cm (½ inch) lengths
ground white pepper, to sprinkle

SERVES 4

TAKE the stems off the dried chillies, cut each chilli into 1 cm (½ inch) pieces with scissors or a sharp knife and discard the seeds.

MIX the fish sauce, oyster sauce, stock and sugar in a small bowl.

HEAT the oil in a wok over a medium heat and stir-fry the cashew nuts for 2 to 3 minutes or until light brown. Remove with a slotted spoon and drain on paper towels.

STIR-FRY the chillies in the same oil over a medium heat for 1 minute. They should darken but not blacken and burn. Remove from the pan with a slotted spoon.

HEAT the same oil again and stir-fry half the garlic over a medium heat until light brown. Add half the chicken and stir-fry over a high heat for 4 to 5 minutes or until the chicken is cooked. Remove from the wok and repeat with the remaining garlic and chicken. Return all the chicken to the wok.

ADD the capsicum, carrot, onion and the sauce mixture to the wok and stir-fry for 1 to 2 minutes. Taste, then adjust the seasoning if necessary.

ADD the cashew nuts, chillies and spring onions and toss well. Sprinkle with ground pepper.

Wat Saen Fang in Chiang Mai.

PHAT THALEH

# MIXED SEAFOOD WITH CHILLIES

THE BIRD'S EYE CHILLIES GIVE THIS DISH QUITE A LOT OF HEAT BUT IF YOU WOULD LIKE IT EVEN HOTTER, JUST ADD A FEW MORE. SERVE WITH PLENTY OF JASMINE RICE AND A COCONUT-BASED CURRY TO HELP TAKE SOME OF THE STING OUT OF THE DISH.

450 g (1 lb) mixed fresh seafood such as prawns (shrimp), squid tubes, small scallops
2 tablespoons vegetable oil
3–4 garlic cloves, finely chopped
1 green capsicum (pepper), cut into bite-sized pieces
1 small onion, cut into thin slices
5 snake beans, cut into 2.5 cm (1 inch) pieces
1 cm (½ inch) piece of ginger, finely grated
4 bird's eye chillies, lightly bruised
1 tablespoon oyster sauce
½ tablespoon light soy sauce
¼ teaspoon sugar
1 long red chilli (optional), seeded and sliced diagonally
1–2 spring onions (scallions), thinly sliced
a few holy basil leaves, or coriander (cilantro) leaves, for garnish

SERVES 4

PEEL and devein the prawns and cut each prawn open along the back so it opens like a butterfly (leave each prawn joined along the base and at the tail). Peel off the outer skin of the squid and rinse out the insides of the tubes. Cut each in half and open the pieces out. Score the inside of each squid with diagonal cuts to make a diamond pattern, then cut into squares. Carefully slice off and discard any vein, membrane or hard white muscle from each scallop. Scallops can be left whole, or, if large, cut each in half.

HEAT the oil in a wok or frying pan and stir-fry the garlic over a medium heat until light brown. Add the capsicum, onion, beans, ginger and chillies and stir-fry for 1 minute.

ADD the seafood in stages, prawns first, then scallops, adding the squid last and tossing after each addition. Add the oyster sauce, light soy sauce and sugar and stir-fry for 2 to 3 minutes, or until the prawns open and turn pink and all the seafood is cooked.

ADD the chilli and spring onions and toss together. Taste, then adjust the seasoning if necessary. Spoon onto a serving plate and sprinkle with basil or coriander leaves.

Mangroves in Phang-nga.

KAI PHAT NAM PHRIK PHAO

# CHICKEN WITH CHILLI JAM

CHILLI JAM, OR ROASTED CHILLI PASTE, IS USED AS A RELISH, CONDIMENT AND INGREDIENT IN VARIOUS THAI DISHES. HERE IT ADDS A MORE COMPLEX SWEET, CHILLI FLAVOUR THAN JUST USING CHILLIES. ADD THE SMALLER AMOUNT BEFORE TASTING, THEN ADD A LITTLE MORE IF YOU NEED TO.

2 teaspoons fish sauce
2 tablespoons oyster sauce
60 ml (¼ cup) coconut milk
    (page 279)
½ teaspoon sugar
2½ tablespoons vegetable oil
6 garlic cloves, finely chopped
1–1½ tablespoons chilli jam
    (page 283), to taste
500 g (1 lb 2 oz) skinless chicken
    breast fillets, finely sliced
a handful of holy basil leaves
1 long red or green chilli,
    seeded and finely sliced,
    for garnish

SERVES 4

MIX the fish sauce, oyster sauce, coconut milk and sugar in a small bowl.

HEAT the oil in a wok or frying pan and stir-fry half the garlic over a medium heat until light brown. Add half the chilli jam and stir-fry for another 2 minutes or until fragrant. Add half of the chicken and stir-fry over a high heat for 2 to 3 minutes. Remove from the wok. Repeat with the remaining garlic, chilli jam and chicken. Return all the chicken to the wok.

ADD the fish sauce mixture to the wok and stir-fry for a few more seconds or until the chicken is cooked. Taste, then adjust the seasoning if necessary. Stir in the basil leaves. Garnish with chilli slices.

Mixing the sauce ingredients together before you start cooking means you can just pour it in when you need to.

Salt harvested from the Gulf of Thailand.

The mushrooms and tofu are cut into similarly sized pieces so that they cook evenly in the wok.

# MUSHROOMS WITH TOFU

TOFU AND MUSHROOMS ARE COMMONLY USED TOGETHER IN CHINESE DISHES, JUST AS THEY ARE HERE IN THIS THAI DISH. THE BLANDNESS OF THE TOFU IS A CONTRAST TO BOTH THE TEXTURE AND FLAVOUR OF THE MUSHROOMS. FOR THE BEST FLAVOUR, USE THE TYPE OF MUSHROOMS SUGGESTED.

350 g (12 oz) firm tofu (bean curd)
1 teaspoon sesame oil
2 teaspoons light soy sauce
¼ teaspoon ground black pepper,
   plus some to sprinkle
1 tablespoon finely shredded ginger
5 tablespoons vegetable stock
   or water
2 tablespoons light soy sauce
2 teaspoons cornflour (cornstarch)
½ teaspoon sugar
1½ tablespoons vegetable oil
2 garlic cloves, finely chopped
200 g (7 oz) oyster mushrooms,
   hard stalks removed, cut in half
   if large
200 g (7 oz) shiitake mushrooms,
   hard stalks removed
2 spring onions (scallions), sliced
   diagonally, for garnish
1 long red chilli, seeded and finely
   sliced, for garnish

SERVES 2

DRAIN each block of tofu and cut into 2.5 cm (1 inch) pieces. Put them in a shallow dish and sprinkle with the sesame oil, light soy sauce, ground pepper and ginger. Leave to marinate for 30 minutes.

MIX the stock with the light soy sauce, cornflour and sugar in a small bowl until smooth.

HEAT the oil in a wok or frying pan and stir-fry the garlic over a medium heat until light brown. Add all the mushrooms and stir-fry for 3 to 4 minutes or until the mushrooms are cooked. Add the cornflour liquid, then carefully add the pieces of tofu and gently mix for 1 to 2 minutes. Taste, then adjust the seasoning if necessary.

SPOON onto a serving plate and sprinkle with spring onions, chilli slices and ground pepper.

Ringing the bells at Wat Phra That Doi Tung.

MUU PHAT KHING

# PORK WITH GINGER

A HYBRID DISH, CHINESE IN STYLE WITH THE ADDITION OF FISH SAUCE FOR A THAI FLAVOUR, THIS RECIPE IS BEST MADE WITH FIRM, YOUNG, TENDER GINGER WITH TRANSLUCENT SKIN. THE AROMA OF THE WHOLE DISH SHOULD BE DISTINCTLY GINGERY AS IT ARRIVES AT THE TABLE.

15 g (½ oz) dried black fungus
  (about half a handful)
1 tablespoon fish sauce
1½ tablespoons oyster sauce
4 tablespoons vegetable or chicken
  stock, or water
½ teaspoon sugar
2 tablespoons vegetable oil
3–4 garlic cloves, finely chopped
500 g (1 lb 2 oz) lean pork,
  finely sliced
25 g (1 oz) ginger, julienned
1 small onion, cut into 8 wedges
2 spring onions (scallions),
  diagonally sliced
ground white pepper, for sprinkling
1 long red chilli, seeded and finely
  sliced, for garnish
a few coriander (cilantro) leaves,
  for garnish

SERVES 4

SOAK the black fungus in hot water for 2 to 3 minutes or until soft, then drain.

MIX the fish sauce, oyster sauce, stock and sugar in a small bowl.

HEAT the oil in a wok or frying pan and stir-fry half the garlic over a medium heat until light brown. Add half the pork and stir-fry over a high heat for 2 to 3 minutes or until the pork is cooked. Remove from the wok. Repeat with the remaining garlic and pork. Return all the pork to the wok.

ADD the ginger, onion, black fungus and the sauce mixture to the wok. Stir-fry for 1 to 2 minutes. Taste, then adjust the seasoning if necessary. Stir in the spring onions.

SPOON onto a serving plate and sprinkle with ground pepper, chilli slices and coriander leaves.

Selling vegetables in Chiang Mai.

# STIR-FRIED GARLIC PRAWNS

TIGER PRAWNS ARE EXTENSIVELY FARMED IN THAILAND AND APPEAR IN MANY DISHES. YOU CAN, HOWEVER, USE DIFFERENT TYPES OF PRAWNS DEPENDING ON AVAILABILITY. THIS RECIPE HAS QUITE A LOT OF GARLIC SO CHOOSE NICE FRESH, SWEET BULBS TO MAKE THE BEST OF THE FLAVOUR.

500 g (1 lb 2 oz) large raw prawns (shrimp)
18–20 coriander (cilantro) roots, roughly chopped
4–5 garlic cloves, roughly chopped
10 black peppercorns
1 tablespoon light soy sauce
1½ tablespoons oyster sauce
½ teaspoon sugar
3 tablespoons vegetable oil
a few coriander (cilantro) leaves, for garnish
1 long red chilli, seeded and finely sliced, for garnish

SERVES 4

PEEL and devein the prawns and cut each prawn along the back so it opens like a butterfly (leave each prawn joined along the base and at the tail).

USING a pestle and mortar or a small blender, pound or grind the coriander roots and garlic into a rough paste. Add the peppercorns and continue to grind roughly.

MIX the light soy sauce, oyster sauce and sugar in a small bowl.

HEAT the oil in a wok or frying pan and stir-fry the coriander paste for 1 to 2 minutes or until the garlic starts to turn light brown and fragrant. Add the prawns and light soy sauce mixture and stir-fry for another 2 to 3 minutes or until the prawns open and turn pink. Taste, then adjust the seasoning if necessary. Sprinkle with coriander leaves and chilli slices.

MUU PHAT PRIAW WAAN

# PORK WITH SWEET AND SOUR SAUCE

PORK IS THE MEAT PREFERRED IN MANY AREAS OF THAILAND. THIS RECIPE IS A THAI VERSION OF THE BETTER KNOWN CHINESE SWEET AND SOUR PORK. THE VEGETABLES CAN BE VARIED ACCORDING TO WHAT IS AVAILABLE, BUT CHOOSE ONES THAT WILL STILL BE CRUNCHY WHEN COOKED.

225 g (8 oz) tin pineapple slices in
   light syrup, each slice cut into
   4 pieces (reserve the syrup)
1½ tablespoons plum sauce
   (page 284) or tomato ketchup
2½ teaspoons fish sauce
1 tablespoon sugar
2 tablespoons vegetable oil
250 g (9 oz) pork, sliced
4 garlic cloves, finely chopped
¼ carrot, sliced
1 medium onion, cut into 8 slices
½ red capsicum (pepper), cut into
   bite-sized pieces
1 small cucumber, unpeeled,
   halved lengthways and cut into
   thick slices
1 tomato, cut into 4 slices, or
   4–5 baby tomatoes
a few coriander (cilantro) leaves,
   for garnish

SERVES 4

MIX all the pineapple syrup (about 6 tablespoons) with the plum sauce, fish sauce and sugar in a small bowl until smooth.

HEAT the oil in a wok or deep frying pan over a medium heat and fry the pork until nicely browned and cooked. Lift out with a slotted spoon and drain on paper towels.

ADD the garlic to the wok or pan and fry over a medium heat for 1 minute or until lightly browned. Add the carrot, onion and capsicum and stir-fry for 1 to 2 minutes. Add the cucumber, tomato, pineapple and pineapple syrup and stir together for another minute. Taste, then adjust the seasoning if necessary.

RETURN the pork to the pan and gently stir. Spoon onto a serving plate and garnish with coriander leaves.

Snake beans sometimes have a mottled dark colouring but this is perfectly normal.

## THUA PHAT MUU
# PORK WITH SNAKE BEANS

SNAKE BEANS ARE SOLD IN ASIAN FOOD SHOPS, EITHER COILED UP OR IN LONG BUNCHES. THEY TASTE SIMILAR TO EUROPEAN GREEN BEANS BUT HAVE A SLIGHTLY MORE LEATHERY SKIN. YOU CAN USE FRENCH OR ROUND GREEN BEANS IF YOU PREFER. THIS DISH GOES WITH ANY MEAL.

1 tablespoon oyster sauce
1 tablespoon light soy sauce
¼ teaspoon sugar
2 tablespoons vegetable oil
4 garlic cloves, finely chopped
350 g (12 oz) pork fillet, finely sliced
250 g (9 oz) snake beans, cut into
   5 cm (2 inch) pieces
½ long red chilli, seeded, shredded,
   for garnish (optional)

SERVES 4

MIX the oyster sauce, light soy sauce, sugar and 2 tablespoons water in a small bowl.

HEAT the oil in a wok or frying pan and stir-fry the garlic over a medium heat until light brown. Add the pork and stir-fry over a high heat for 3 to 5 minutes or until the pork is cooked. Add the beans and the sauce mixture and stir-fry for 4 minutes. Taste, then adjust the seasoning if necessary.

TRANSFER to a serving plate and garnish with chilli slices.

MUU PHAT KRA-TIAM PHRIK THAI

# PORK WITH GARLIC AND PEPPER

A CLASSIC COMBINATION OF GARLIC AND PEPPER IS FOUND IN THIS CHINESE-STYLE DISH. THAI GARLIC IS LESS PUNGENT THAN MANY OTHER GARLICS. TRY TO BUY NEW SEASON GARLIC. CRUSH THE PEPPERCORNS JUST BEFORE YOU USE THEM. SERVE WITH A VEGETABLE DISH AND JASMINE RICE.

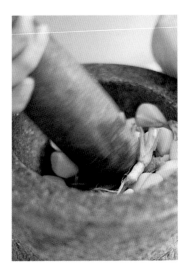

1½ teaspoons black peppercorns
1 whole bulb of garlic, cloves
    roughly chopped
8–10 coriander (cilantro) roots,
    roughly chopped
3 tablespoons vegetable oil
500 g (1 lb 2 oz) pork fillet, cut into
    5 cm (2 inch) squares
1 tablespoon fish sauce
1 tablespoon light soy sauce
½ teaspoon sugar
garlic and chilli sauce (page 283),
    to serve

SERVES 4

USING a pestle and mortar or a small blender, pound or blend the black peppercorns (just roughly) and spoon them into a small bowl.

POUND or blend the garlic and coriander roots into a paste and mix with peppercorns.

HEAT the oil in a wok or frying pan and stir-fry half the garlic and peppercorn paste over a medium heat for 1 to 2 minutes or until the garlic turns light brown and is fragrant. Add half the pork and stir-fry over a high heat for a minute, then reduce the heat and cook for 2 to 3 minutes, or until the meat is cooked. Remove from the heat. Repeat with the remaining paste and pork. Return all the pork to the wok.

ADD the fish sauce, light soy sauce and sugar to the wok. Stir-fry for 5 minutes or until the pork starts to turn brown. Serve with garlic and chilli sauce.

A granite pestle and mortar helps in many Thai recipes. A deep mortar is best when you have a lot of ingredients.

Chillies and garlic at a Bangkok market.

# NOODLES & RICE

Stir the paste into the coconut cream before adding the chicken, soy sauce, sugar, stock and coconut milk.

# CHIANG MAI NOODLES

ONE OF CHIANG MAI'S WELL KNOWN DISHES, THIS IS FOUND ON RESTAURANT MENUS AND AT HAWKER STALLS, PARTICULARLY THOSE NEAR THE MOSQUE. SERVE WITH THE ACCOMPANIMENTS SUGGESTED AS THEY COMPLEMENT THE NOODLES PARTICULARLY WELL.

### PASTE
3 dried long red chillies
4 Asian shallots, chopped
4 garlic cloves, crushed
2 cm (¾ inch) piece of turmeric, grated
5 cm (2 inch) piece of ginger, grated
4 tablespoons chopped coriander (cilantro) roots
1 teaspoon shrimp paste
1 teaspoon curry powder (page 287)

5 tablespoons coconut cream (page 279)
2 tablespoons palm sugar
2 tablespoons soy sauce
4 chicken drumsticks and 4 chicken thighs, with skin and bone
500 ml (2 cups) chicken stock or water
410 ml (1⅔ cups) coconut milk (page 279)
400 g (14 oz) fresh flat egg noodles
chopped or sliced spring onions (scallions), for garnish
a handful of coriander (cilantro) leaves, for garnish
lime wedges, to serve
pickled mustard greens or cucumber, to serve
roasted chilli sauce (page 283), to serve
Asian shallots, quartered, to serve

SERVES 4

TO MAKE the paste, soak the dried chillies in hot water for 10 minutes, then drain and chop the chillies into pieces, discarding the seeds. Put the chillies in a pestle and mortar with the shallots, garlic, turmeric, ginger, coriander roots and shrimp paste and pound to a fine paste. Add the curry powder and a pinch of salt and mix well.

PUT the coconut cream in a wok or saucepan and simmer over a medium heat for about 5 minutes, or until the cream separates and a layer of oil forms on the surface. Stir the cream if it starts to brown around the edges.

ADD the paste and stir until fragrant. Add the palm sugar, soy sauce and chicken and stir well, then add the stock and coconut milk and bring to the boil. Reduce the heat and simmer for 30 minutes or until the chicken is cooked and tender.

MEANWHILE, cook 100 g (3 oz) of the egg noodles by deep-frying them in very hot oil in a saucepan until they puff up. Drain on paper towels. Cook the remaining noodles in boiling water according to the packet instructions.

PUT the boiled noodles in a large bowl and spoon the chicken mixture over the top. Garnish with the crispy noodles, spring onions and coriander leaves. Serve the accompaniments alongside.

KIAW NAAM KUNG

# WON TON SOUP WITH PRAWNS

WON TONS ARE A CHINESE-STYLE STUFFED NOODLE. USUALLY SERVED IN SOUPS, THEY ARE EASY TO

PREPARE, AND WITH THIS LIGHT, FRESH PRAWN FILLING WON TONS MAKE A GOOD MEAL IN A BOWL

AT ANY TIME OF DAY. CHICKEN OR FISH ARE ALSO SUITABLE FILLINGS.

225 g (8 oz) finely chopped prawns
  (shrimp)
6 garlic cloves, finely chopped
2 coriander (cilantro) roots,
  finely chopped
a sprinkle of ground white pepper
20 won ton sheets 7.5 cm
  (3 inches) square
1–2 tablespoons vegetable oil
935 ml (3¾ cups) chicken or
  vegetable stock
2 tablespoons light soy sauce
4 raw prawns (shrimp), peeled
  and deveined
100 g (4 oz) Chinese cabbage or
  spinach leaves, roughly chopped
100 g (1 cup) bean sprouts, tails
  removed
3 spring onions (scallions), slivered
ground white pepper, for sprinkling

SERVES 4

IN a bowl, combine the chopped prawns with
2 of the garlic cloves, the coriander roots, ground
pepper and a pinch of salt. Spoon 1 teaspoon of
the mixture into the middle of each won ton sheet.
Gather up, squeezing the corners together to
make a little purse.

HEAT the oil in a small wok or frying pan and stir-
fry the remaining garlic until light golden. Remove
from the heat and discard the garlic.

HEAT a saucepan of water to boiling point. Gently
drop each won ton purse into the water and
cook for 2 to 3 minutes. Lift each purse out
with a slotted spoon and drop it into a bowl of
warm water.

HEAT the stock in a saucepan to boiling point.
Add the light soy sauce, prawns and Chinese
cabbage and cook for a few minutes.

DRAIN the cooked won tons and transfer them
to the stock saucepan.

DIVIDE the bean sprouts among individual bowls
and divide the won tons and the soup mixture
among the bowls. Garnish with spring onions,
ground pepper and the garlic oil.

Spoon a small amount of mixture
onto each won ton sheet, gather
up and squeeze into a purse.

Score the insides of the squid tubes in a crisscross pattern.

Preparing fish in Phetchaburi.

# EGG NOODLES WITH SEAFOOD

BA-MII ARE WHEAT FLOUR NOODLES, USUALLY MADE WITH EGG. STALLS SPECIALIZING IN BA-MII CAN BE FOUND ALL OVER THAILAND — NOODLE DISHES LIKE THIS ARE USUALLY EATEN AS A SNACK. SERVE WITH SLICED CHILLIES IN FISH SAUCE, DRIED CHILLI AND WHITE SUGAR FOR SEASONING.

8 raw prawns (shrimp)
2 squid tubes
250 g (9 oz) egg noodles
1 tablespoon vegetable oil
4 Asian shallots, smashed with the side of a cleaver
4 spring onions (scallions), cut into lengths and smashed with the side of a cleaver
2 cm (¾ inch) piece of ginger, finely shredded
2 garlic cloves, finely sliced
1 tablespoon preserved cabbage, rinsed and chopped (optional)
4 scallops, cut in half horizontally
1 tablespoon oyster sauce
2 teaspoons soy sauce
2 teaspoons fish sauce
½ bunch (1 cup) holy basil leaves

SERVES 4

PEEL and devein the prawns and cut each prawn along the back so it opens like a butterfly (leave each prawn joined along the base and at the tail, leaving the tail attached).

OPEN out the squid tubes and score the insides in a criss-cross pattern. Cut the squid tubes into squares.

COOK the egg noodles in boiling water, then drain and rinse.

HEAT the oil in a wok and add the shallots, spring onions, ginger, garlic and cabbage and stir-fry for 2 minutes. Add the prawns, squid and scallops one after the other, tossing after each addition, and cook for 3 minutes.

ADD the oyster and soy sauces and noodles and toss together. Add the fish sauce and holy basil and serve.

## PHAT WUN SEN
# HOT AND SOUR NOODLES WITH PRAWNS

200 g (7 oz) mung bean vermicelli
100 g (3 oz) minced (ground) pork
2 tablespoons oil
8 cooked prawns (shrimp), peeled
4 pickled garlic cloves, chopped
2 Asian shallots, finely sliced
4 bird's eye chillies, finely sliced
2 tablespoons fish sauce
1 tablespoon lime juice
2 tomatoes, seeded and cut into
    thin wedges
½ bunch (1 cup) Thai sweet basil
    leaves
½ bunch (1 cup) coriander (cilantro)
    leaves

SERVES 4

SOAK the noodles in hot water for 10 minutes or until soft. Drain the noodles and cut them into shorter lengths using a pair of scissors.

COOK the pork in boiling water for 2 minutes, breaking it up into small pieces, then drain.

HEAT the oil in a wok and add all the ingredients except the basil and coriander. Toss together for a minute or two. Add the herbs, toss briefly and serve.

Toss all the ingredients together before adding the herbs.

## KUAYTIAW PHAT KHII MAO
# STIR-FRIED NOODLES WITH HOLY BASIL

NOODLES ARE ONE OF THE MOST COMMON DISHES IN THAILAND, FOUND ON JUST ABOUT EVERY STREET CORNER. AS THEY ARE OF CHINESE ORIGIN THEY ARE USUALLY EATEN OUT OF A BOWL WITH CHOPSTICKS AND A SPOON. SERVE STRAIGHT OUT OF THE WOK.

450 g (1 lb) wide fresh flat rice
    noodles (sen yai)
2 teaspoons soy sauce
4 garlic cloves
4 bird's eye chillies, stems removed
4 tablespoons vegetable oil
200 g (7 oz) skinless chicken fillets,
    cut into thin strips
2 tablespoons fish sauce
2 teaspoons palm sugar
½ bunch (1 cup) holy basil leaves

SERVES 4

PUT the noodles in a bowl with the soy sauce and rub the sauce through the noodles, separating them out as you do so. Pound the garlic and chillies together with a pestle and mortar until you have a fine paste.

HEAT the oil in a wok and add the garlic and chilli paste and fry until fragrant. Add the chicken and toss until cooked. Add the fish sauce and palm sugar and cook until the sugar dissolves. Add the noodles and basil leaves, toss together and serve.

STIR-FRIED NOODLES WITH
HOLY BASIL

Pound the flavours into a paste.
Cook for a few minutes, then
add the rice and, when coated,
transfer to a clay pot.

Painting umbrellas at Bo Sang
village.

KUNG LAI SAI KRAWK NAI MAW DIN

# PRAWNS AND SAUSAGE IN A CLAY POT

CLAY POT COOKING IS CHINESE IN STYLE. IF YOU HAVE FOUR SMALLER CLAY POTS YOU CAN MAKE INDIVIDUAL DISHES TO SERVE INSTEAD OF ONE LARGE ONE. A HEAVY CASSEROLE WILL WORK JUST AS WELL. THE INGREDIENTS IN THE DISH WILL FLAVOUR THE RICE AS IT COOKS.

12 raw small prawns (shrimp),
 peeled, deveined and roughly
 chopped
1 lemon grass stalk, white part only,
 finely chopped
2 large green chillies, chopped
1 teaspoon Thai whisky or rice wine
1 teaspoon fish sauce
1 teaspoon tapioca flour
2 garlic cloves, chopped
2 coriander (cilantro) roots, chopped
2 cm (¾ inch) piece of ginger,
 chopped
2 Asian shallots, chopped
200 g (1 cup) jasmine rice
2 tablespoons oil
2 Thai or Chinese sour sausages,
 finely sliced
2 tablespoons chopped coriander
 (cilantro), for garnish

SERVES 4

PUT the chopped prawns in a bowl with
1 tablespoon of lemon grass, the chillies, whisky,
fish sauce and tapioca flour. Stir to combine.

POUND the remaining lemon grass, garlic,
coriander roots, ginger and shallots in a pestle
and mortar or blend in a small food processor
to form a rough paste.

WASH the rice in cold water until the water runs
clear, then drain.

HEAT the oil in a wok, add the garlic paste and
cook for 3 to 4 minutes, stirring constantly. Add
the rice and cook for a minute to coat the rice
evenly in the mixture.

TRANSFER the rice into a large clay pot and add
water so there is 2 cm (¾ inch) of water above the
surface of the rice. Bring the water to a slow boil,
then place the sausage slices on top of the rice
and the prawn mixture on top of the sausages.
Cover the clay pot and cook over a low heat for
15 minutes or until the rice is cooked. Serve
sprinkled with the chopped coriander.

PHAT KUAYTIAW RAAT NAA MUU

# STIR-FRIED WHITE NOODLES WITH PORK

NOODLES ARE ENJOYED WITH FERVOUR IN THAILAND. LARGE WHITE NOODLES ARE USED IN THIS DISH, WHICH IS ONE OF THE BEST-KNOWN NOODLE DISHES, SERVED AT ANY TIME OF THE DAY OR NIGHT. THE LIGHT, BITTER TASTE COMES FROM THE CHINESE KALE.

2 teaspoons oyster sauce
6 teaspoons light soy sauce
1 teaspoon sugar
2 teaspoons yellow bean sauce
1 tablespoon tapioca flour
450 g (1 lb) wide fresh flat rice
    noodles *(sen yai)*
4 tablespoons vegetable oil
4–5 garlic cloves, finely chopped
225 g (8 oz) pork or chicken fillet,
    finely sliced
175 g (6 oz) Chinese kale, cut into
    2.5 cm (1 inch) pieces, leaves
    separated
ground white pepper, for sprinkling

SEASONING
6 bird's eye chillies, sliced and
    mixed with 3 tablespoons
    white vinegar
3 tablespoons fish sauce
3 tablespoons roasted chilli powder
3 tablespoons white sugar

SERVES 4

MIX the oyster sauce, 4 teaspoons of the light soy sauce, sugar, yellow bean sauce and tapioca flour with 125 ml (½ cup) water in a bowl.

PUT the noodles in a bowl with 2 teaspoons of the soy sauce and rub the sauce through the noodles, separating them out as you do so.

HEAT 2 tablespoons oil in a wok or frying pan over a medium heat and stir-fry the noodles for 4 to 5 minutes or until the noodles are browning at the edges and beginning to stick. Keep them warm on a serving plate.

HEAT the remaining oil in a wok or frying pan and stir-fry the garlic over a medium heat until light brown. Add the pork and stir-fry for 2 to 3 minutes or until the meat is cooked. Add the stalks of Chinese kale and stir-fry for 1 to 2 minutes. Add the sauce mixture and the top leaves and stir together for another minute or so. Taste and adjust the seasoning if necessary.

SPOON the pork and Chinese kale on top of the noodles and sprinkle with white pepper. Serve the seasoning ingredients in small bowls on the side, for adjusting the flavour.

Stir-fry the noodles, then remove and stir-fry the garlic, pork and Chinese kale stalks. Add the sauce and kale leaves.

This melding of flavours with noodles is popular in Thailand.

# THAI FRIED NOODLES WITH PRAWNS

THIS IS ONE OF THE MOST FAMOUS DISHES IN THAILAND. EVERYONE WHO VISITS SHOULD TRY IT, OTHERWISE THEY HAVE NOT REALLY BEEN THERE AT ALL. TO MAKE IT, YOU NEED TO USE SMALL WHITE NOODLES OF THE DRIED SEN LEK VARIETY. YOU CAN SUBSTITUTE MEAT FOR PRAWNS.

150 g (5 oz) dried noodles *(sen lek)*
300 g (10 oz) raw large prawns
  (shrimp)
3 tablespoons tamarind purée
2½ tablespoons fish sauce
2 tablespoons palm sugar
3 tablespoons vegetable oil
3–4 garlic cloves, finely chopped
2 eggs
85 g (3 oz) Chinese chives
  (1 bunch)
¼ teaspoon chilli powder,
  depending on taste
2 tablespoons dried shrimp, ground
  or pounded
2 tablespoons preserved turnip,
  finely chopped
2½–3 tablespoons chopped
  roasted peanuts
180 g (2 cups) bean sprouts
3 spring onions (scallions), slivered
1 long red chilli, seeded and
  shredded, for garnish
a few coriander (cilantro) leaves,
  for garnish
lime wedges, to serve

SERVES 4

SOAK the noodles in hot water for 1 to 2 minutes or until soft, then drain.

PEEL and devein the prawns and cut each prawn along the back so it opens like a butterfly (leave each prawn joined along the base and at the tail, leaving the tail attached).

COMBINE the tamarind with the fish sauce and palm sugar in a bowl.

HEAT 1½ tablespoons oil in a wok or frying pan and stir-fry the garlic over a medium heat until light brown. Add the prawns and cook for 2 minutes.

USING a spatula, move the prawns out from the middle of the wok. Add another 1½ tablespoons oil to the wok. Add the eggs and stir to scramble for 1 minute. Add the noodles and chives and stir-fry for a few seconds. Add the fish sauce mixture, chilli powder, dried shrimp, preserved turnip and half of the peanuts. Add half of the bean sprouts and spring onions. Test the noodles for tenderness and adjust the seasoning if necessary.

SPOON onto the serving plate and sprinkle the remaining peanuts over the top. Garnish with shredded chillies and a few coriander leaves. Place the lime wedges and remaining bean sprouts and spring onions at the side of the dish.

MII KROB

# CRISPY RICE NOODLES

THIS IS MADE BY DEEP-FRYING THE THINNEST RICE NOODLES INTO LIGHT AND CRISPY TANGLES. THESE ARE THEN TOSSED WITH SWEET AND SOUR SAUCE. THIS DISH SHOULD BE SERVED AS SOON AS IT IS COOKED OR THE NOODLES WILL LOSE THEIR CRISPINESS.

75 g (3 oz) rice vermicelli noodles (sen mii)

vegetable oil, for deep-frying

200 g (7 oz) firm tofu (bean curd), cut into matchsticks

75 g (3 oz) small Asian shallots or small red onions, finely sliced

150 g (5 oz) raw prawns (shrimp), peeled and deveined, tails intact

2 tablespoons fish sauce

2 tablespoons water or pickled garlic juice

1 tablespoon lime juice

2 tablespoons plum sauce (page 284) or tomato ketchup

1 tablespoon sweet chilli sauce (page 284)

4 tablespoons sugar

3 tablespoons palm sugar

3 small whole pickled garlic, finely sliced

110 g (1¼ cups) bean sprouts, tails removed, for garnish

3–4 spring onions (scallions), slivered, for garnish

1 long red chilli, seeded and cut into slivers, for garnish

SERVES 4

SOAK the noodles in cold water for 20 minutes, drain and dry very thoroughly on paper towels. Cut them into smaller lengths with a pair of scissors.

PUT the oil in the wok to a depth of about 8–10 cm (3–4 inches) and heat over a medium heat. Drop a piece of noodle into the wok. If it sinks and then immediately floats and puffs, the oil is ready. Drop a small handful of the noodles into the oil. Turn them once (it only takes seconds) and remove them as soon as they have swelled and turned a dark ivory colour. Remove the crispy noodles with a slotted spoon, hold over the wok briefly to drain, then transfer to a baking tray lined with paper towels to drain. Fry the remaining noodles in the same way. Break into smaller bits.

IN the same oil, deep-fry the tofu for 7 to 10 minutes or until golden and crisp. Remove and drain with a slotted spoon.

DEEP-FRY the shallots until crispy and golden brown. Remove with a slotted spoon and drain on paper towels.

DEEP-FRY the prawns for 1 to 2 minutes until they turn pink. Remove with a slotted spoon and drain on paper towels.

CAREFULLY pour off all the oil in the wok. Add the fish sauce, water, lime juice, plum sauce, sweet chilli sauce, sugar and palm sugar to the wok. Stir for 4 to 5 minutes over a low heat until slightly thick.

ADD half of the rice noodles and toss gently, mixing them into the sauce. Add the remaining noodles and tofu, prawns, pickled garlic and the shallots, tossing for 1 to 2 minutes until coated. Spoon onto a platter and garnish with bean sprouts, spring onions and chilli slivers.

Thai pickled garlic can be bought from Thai and Asian shops. Remove the crispy noodles and tofu with a slotted spoon.

PHAT BA-MII PHAK

# STIR-FRIED EGG NOODLES WITH VEGETABLES

2 tablespoons oyster sauce
1 tablespoon light soy sauce
1 teaspoon sugar
2 tablespoons vegetable oil
4 garlic cloves, finely chopped
225 g (8 oz) mixed Chinese broccoli
    florets, baby sweet corn,
    snake beans cut into lengths,
    snow peas (mangetout) cut into
    bite-sized pieces
250 g (9 oz) fresh egg noodles
45 g (½ cup) bean sprouts
3 spring onions (scallions), finely
    chopped
½ long red or green chilli, seeded
    and finely sliced
a few coriander (cilantro) leaves,
    for garnish

SERVES 4

COMBINE the oyster sauce, light soy sauce and sugar in a small bowl.

HEAT the oil in a wok or frying pan and stir-fry the garlic over a medium heat until lightly brown. Add all the mixed vegetables and stir-fry over a high heat for 1 to 2 minutes.

ADD the egg noodles and oyster sauce mixture to the wok and stir-fry for 2 to 3 minutes. Add the bean sprouts and spring onions. Taste, then adjust the seasoning if necessary.

SPOON onto a serving plate and garnish with chilli and coriander leaves.

KHAO PHAT KUNG NAAM PHRIK PHAO

# FRIED RICE WITH PRAWNS AND CHILLI JAM

225 g (8 oz) raw prawns (shrimp)
3 tablespoons vegetable oil
4 garlic cloves, finely chopped
1 small onion, sliced
3 teaspoons chilli jam (page 283)
450 g (1 lb) cooked jasmine rice,
    refrigerated overnight
1 tablespoon light soy sauce
½ teaspoon sugar
1 long red chilli, seeded and
    finely sliced
2 spring onions (scallions),
    finely sliced
ground white pepper, for sprinkling
a few coriander (cilantro) leaves,
    for garnish

SERVES 4

PEEL and devein the prawns and cut each prawn along the back so it opens like a butterfly (leave each prawn joined along the base and at the tail, leaving the tail attached).

HEAT the oil in a wok or frying pan and stir-fry the garlic and onion over a medium heat until light brown. Add the chilli jam and stir for a few seconds or until fragrant. Add the prawns and stir-fry over a high heat for 2 minutes or until the prawns open and turn pink.

ADD the cooked rice, light soy sauce and sugar and stir-fry for 3 to 4 minutes. Add the chilli and spring onions and mix well. Taste, then adjust the seasoning if necessary.

SPOON onto a serving place and sprinkle with the white pepper and coriander leaves.

KHAO PHAT SAPPAROT
# FRIED RICE WITH PINEAPPLE

FRIED RICE ORIGINATED IN CHINA AND IS NOW A STAPLE SNACK IN THAILAND. IT IS NOT EATEN INSTEAD OF STEAMED RICE BUT ON ITS OWN. THIS IS A UNIQUE WAY OF PRESENTING FRIED RICE. IT IS A SPLENDID DISH TO SERVE WHEN PINEAPPLES ARE IN SEASON AND EASY TO FIND.

1 fresh pineapple, leaves attached
2 tablespoons vegetable oil
1 egg, beaten with a pinch of salt
2–3 garlic cloves, finely chopped
150 g (5 oz) raw prawns (shrimp),
    peeled and deveined
150 g (5 oz) ham, finely chopped
25 g (1 oz) sweet corn kernels
25 g (1 oz) peas
½ red capsicum (pepper),
    finely diced
1 tablespoon finely sliced ginger
    (optional)
280 g (1½ cups) cooked jasmine
    rice, refrigerated overnight
1 tablespoon light soy sauce
25 g (1 oz) ready-made roasted
    salted cashew nuts,
    roughly chopped
1 long red chilli, seeded and finely
    sliced, for garnish
a few coriander (cilantro) leaves,
    for garnish

SERVES 4

Carefully scoop out flesh of the pineapple leaving a shell for the fried rice filling.

PREHEAT the oven to 180°C/350°F/Gas 4. Cut the pineapple in half, lengthways. Scoop the flesh out of both halves using a tablespoon and a paring knife, to leave two shells with a 1 cm (½ inch) border of flesh attached. Cut the pineapple flesh into small cubes. Put half the cubes in a bowl and refrigerate the rest for eating later.

WRAP the pineapple leaves in foil to prevent them from burning. Place the shells on a baking tray and bake for 10 to 15 minutes. This will seal in the juice and prevent it leaking into the fried rice when it is placed in the shells.

HEAT 1 tablespoon oil in a wok or frying pan over a medium heat. Pour in the egg and swirl the pan so that the egg coats it, forming a thin omelette. Cook for 2 minutes, or until the egg is set and slightly brown on the underside, then flip over to brown the other side. Remove from the pan and allow to cool slightly. Roll up and cut into thin strips.

HEAT 1 tablespoon oil in the wok or frying pan and stir-fry the garlic over a medium heat until light brown. Add the prawns, ham, sweet corn, peas, capsicum and ginger. Stir-fry for 2 minutes or until the prawns open and turn pink. Add the cooked rice, light soy sauce and the bowl of fresh pineapple and toss together over a medium heat for 5 to 7 minutes. Taste, then adjust the seasoning if necessary.

SPOON as much of the fried rice as will fit into the pineapple shells and sprinkle with cashew nuts and omelette strips. Garnish with sliced chillies and coriander leaves.

Fresh and pickled fruit in Udon Thani.

# HOT AND SOUR SOUP WITH NOODLES AND PRAWNS

THIS IS A TANGY SOUP VERSION OF A NOODLE SALAD. WUN SEN NOODLES ARE MADE FROM MUNG BEANS. THEY TURN CLEAR WHEN SOAKED AND ADD A SLIPPERY TEXTURE TO THIS SOUP. CUT THE NOODLES INTO SMALL PIECES TO MAKE THEM EASIER TO EAT.

150 g (5 oz) vermicelli or mung bean vermicelli (*wun sen*)

280 g (10 oz) raw medium prawns (shrimp)

920 ml (3⅔ cups) vegetable stock

2 lemon grass stalks, each cut into a tassel or bruised

2–2½ tablespoons fish sauce

1½–2 tablespoons chilli jam (page 283), depending on taste (optional)

1–2 small red and green chillies, slightly crushed

110 g (4 oz) mixed mushrooms

110 g (4 oz) baby tomatoes (about 10) or medium tomatoes, cut into 6 pieces

5 makrut (kaffir) lime leaves, torn in half

4 tablespoons lime juice

a few coriander (cilantro) leaves, for garnish

SERVES 4

SOAK the vermicelli in hot water for 1 to 2 minutes or until soft, then drain them well and cut into small pieces.

PEEL and devein the prawns and cut each prawn along the back so it opens like a butterfly (leave each prawn joined along the base and at the tail, leaving the tail attached).

HEAT the stock, lemon grass, fish sauce, chilli jam and crushed chillies to boiling point. Reduce the heat to medium, add the vermicelli, then cook for 1 to 2 minutes. Add the prawns and cook for another minute.

ADD the mushrooms, tomatoes, makrut lime leaves and lime juice. Cook for another 2 to 3 minutes, taking care not to let the tomatoes lose their shape. Taste, then adjust the seasoning if necessary. Discard the lemon grass. Spoon into a bowl and garnish with coriander leaves.

KHAO PHAT PUU

# FRIED RICE WITH CRAB

FRIED RICE IS BEST MADE WITH DAY-OLD RICE, IN OTHER WORDS LEFTOVERS, THOUGH THE LIKELIHOOD OF THERE BEING LEFTOVER RICE IN THAILAND IS REMOTE. USE A WOK FOR THE BEST RESULTS. CRAB, PREFERABLY FRESH IF POSSIBLE, GOES PARTICULARLY WELL WITH THE RICE.

Fresh water chestnuts.

2 tablespoons vegetable oil
4 garlic cloves, finely chopped
2 eggs
450 g (2½ cups) cooked jasmine
   rice, refrigerated overnight
110 g (4 oz) crab meat
   (drained well if tinned)
½ small onion, sliced
175 g (6 oz) tin water chestnuts,
   drained and sliced
2 tablespoons finely julienned ginger
   (optional)
1 tablespoon light soy sauce
1 teaspoon sugar
4 cooked crab claws, for garnish
½ long red chilli, seeded and finely
   sliced, for garnish
2 spring onions (scallions), finely
   chopped, for garnish

SERVES 4

HEAT the oil in a wok or frying pan and stir-fry the garlic over a medium heat until light brown. Using a spatula, move the fried garlic to the outer edges of the wok. Add the eggs and stir to scramble for 1 to 2 minutes. Add the cooked rice, crab meat and onion, stirring for 1 to 2 minutes.

ADD the water chestnuts, ginger, light soy sauce and sugar and stir together for 1 minute. Taste, then adjust the seasoning if necessary.

SPOON onto a serving plate and garnish with the crab claws. Sprinkle with sliced chilli and spring onions.

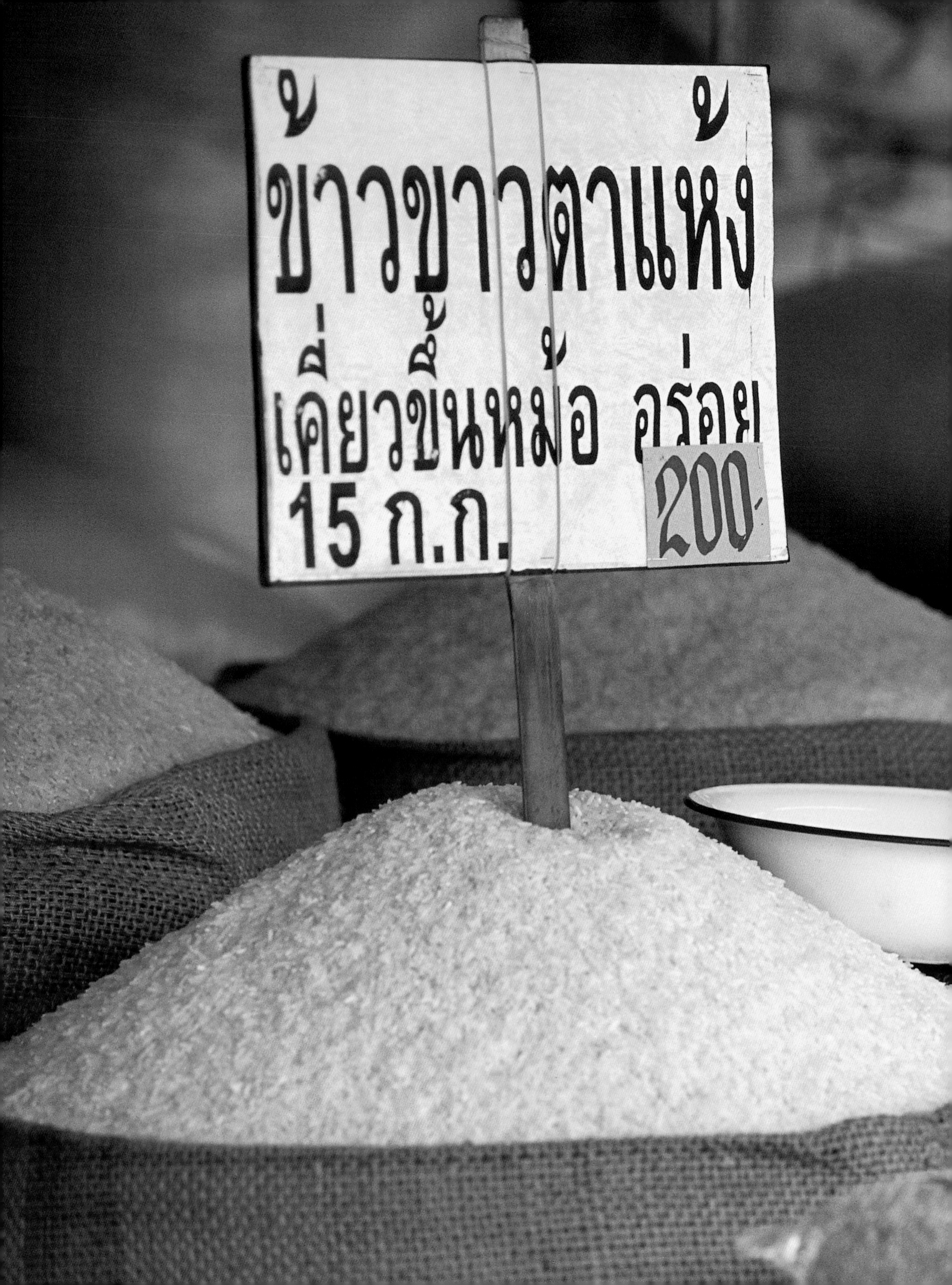
ข้าวขาวตาแห้ง
เคี่ยวขึ้นหม้อ อร่อย
15 ก.ก.
200-

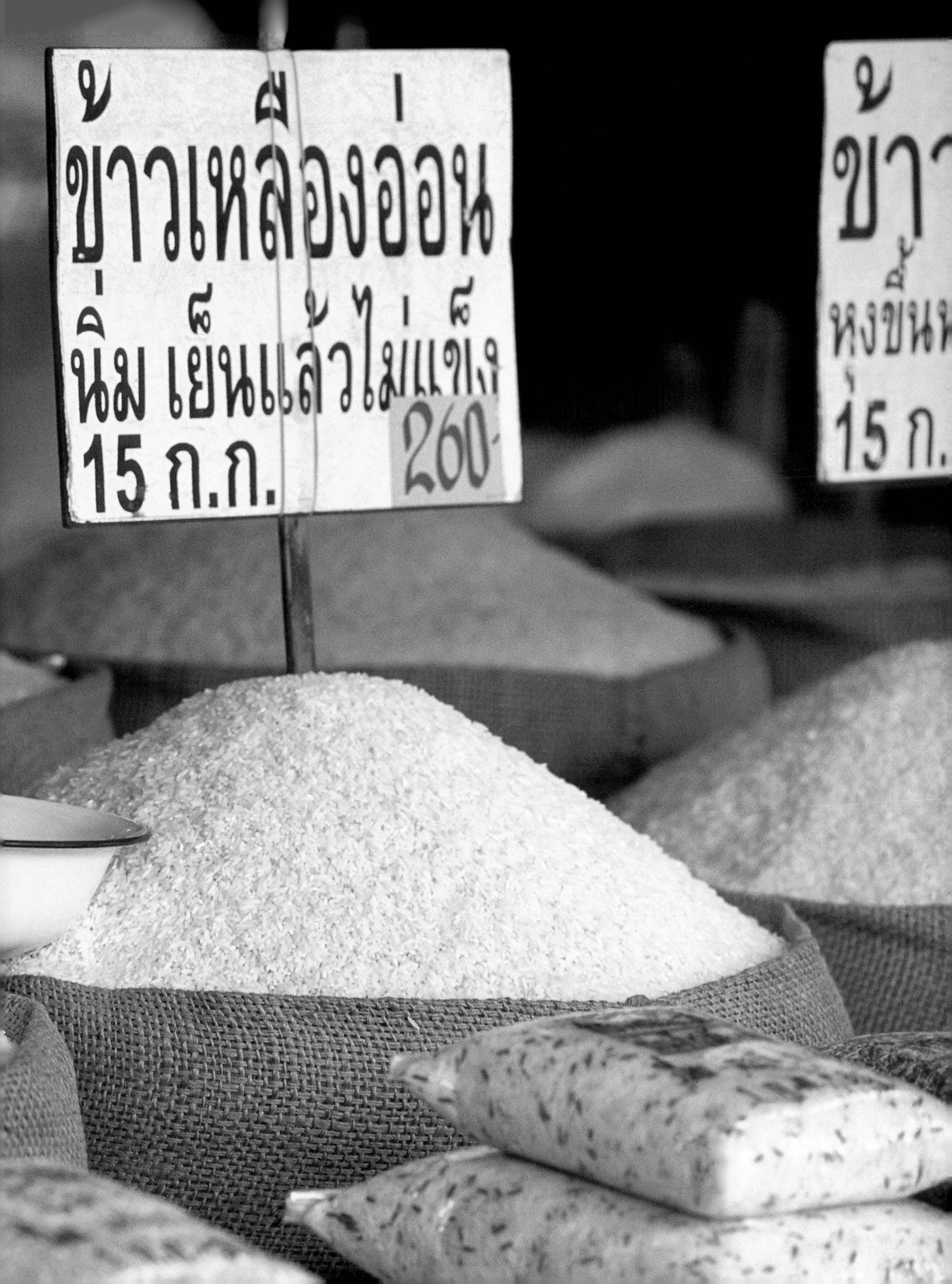
ข้าวเหลืองอ่อน
นิ่ม เย็นแล้วไม่แข็ง
15 ก.ก.
260-
ข้าว
หุงขึ้น
15 ก.

COMMERCIAL RICE GROWING Rather than investing in large expanses of land on which to grow rice, many rice companies buy unhusked rice from farmers surrounding their mills. Once harvested, the rice is bagged up and taken to the mill to be tested: if it is good quality it is bought by the mill and processed. At the Chia Meng rice mill it is tested for ripeness and for the percentage of jasmine or fragrant rice in the

# RICE

RICE (KHAO) IS NOT ONLY THE STAPLE FOOD OF THAILAND, IT IS A FUNDAMENTAL PART OF THAI LIFE, INTEGRAL TO ITS CULTURE AND TRADITIONS. THE GREETING KIN KHAO LAEW REU YANG MEANS 'HOW ARE YOU' BUT IS TRANSLATED AS 'HAVE YOU EATEN RICE YET?'. RICE IS NOT JUST PART OF A MEAL, IT IS THE MEAL. OTHER DISHES ARE ACCOMPANIMENTS.

The cultivation of rice may have started in Thailand. Wild rice originated somewhere in an area that now runs through Upper Assam, Burma, northern Thailand, South-West China and northern Vietnam, a fertile belt that is given over to rice cultivation today. The indigenous inhabitants of the area, were cultivating rice in what would eventually become part of the kingdom of Thailand at a time when most of China was still eating millet. The cultivation of rice led to settlements of people as paddy fields needed supervising.

Rice became important to the Thai economy as it became a staple elsewhere. Arab and Indian traders took rice to India and the Middle East and the Chinese absorbed rice into the cuisine until it became their staple as well. Rice also travelled throughout South-East Asia. Thailand is one of the world's major rice exporters and is self sufficient in this staple food.

## TYPES OF RICE

Most of the rice eaten in Thailand comes from local paddy. Originally, sticky rice was predominant but gradually long-grain rice became popular. The North and North-East still

RICE NOODLES Rice is also used to make kuaytiaw or rice noodles. Rice flour is mixed with water, then this paste is spread out in trays and steamed before being cut into different widths. Wide noodles are sen yai or wide line, medium are sen lek or small line, and thin noodles are sen mii, line noodles. Rice noodles are sold fresh in markets or dried in packets and are used in soups or stir-fried and eaten with sauces.

mix. The rice is dried by spreading it out in the sun and is then cleaned of impurities, husked, polished and sorted into broken and whole grains. It is finally sieved to sort it into different sizes before being bagged. Broken and smaller grained rices are sold locally. New crop rice is often exported to Singapore, and older, harder rice to Hong Kong. Local companies may mix new and old rice to give a 'perfect' mix.

prefer sticky rice but elsewhere long-grain is more common. Sticky rice is also used for desserts in both its white and 'black' forms. Long-grain rice is served with every meal except snacks. A spoonful is usually eaten by itself before any other dish is added to it and it is never swamped with other food. Sticky rice is eaten by rolling some rice into a ball with one hand. It is then used to pick up food or to dip into a sauce. It is always eaten using your hand.

## QUALITY

The quality of rice is of paramount importance to the Thais. Jasmine rice, which has a flowery fragrance, is considered to be the best variety of long-grain. Like wine connoisseurs, some Thais can tell how old rice is, and how and where it was grown. Rice is generally eaten within 12 to 18 months of harvesting. It is at its best after three months because when it is very new and still high in moisture, it is stickier. The drier rice becomes, the more water it needs to be cooked in.

**STICKY RICE** Sticky rice is often cooked in a container or wrapping. It is soaked in water overnight and then pushed into lengths of bamboo that are plugged at one end. Coconut milk mixed with salt and sugar is added and the bamboo then grilled over coals. Little parcels of sticky rice are also steamed in leaves. Banana, coconut and lotus leaves are all used as wrappings.

**HILL TRIBE RICE** Rice is cut and threshed by hand by the hill tribes of northern Thailand. The harvested rice is gathered up between two sticks and threshed against the sides of a giant woven bowl until the rice grains are shaken loose from the stalks. The grains are then tossed in the air and fanned, to blow away as much chaff as possible, before being transferred to a flat area where it is raked out and dried in the sun.

## CULTIVATION

Rice is cultivated in several different ways depending on the area in which it is grown. An average crop of rice takes between 100 and 200 days to mature depending on variety and growing climate. Quick-maturing crops give some areas two rice harvests a year and in other regions quick and slow growing crops are planted together to string out the harvest and make it more manageable.

Rice can be grown in paddy fields — that is, in water — or in fields that are dry except for rainfall. Rice that relies on rainfall is mainly grown by hill tribes in northern Thailand. These farmers rotate their fields as the land becomes exhausted, cutting down new areas of jungle as they need them.

Technology is relatively primitive in these areas and there are few labour-saving devices. Families within each tribal group help each other. Planting takes place in the monsoon season, July to October, and sometimes in November.

Paddy rice is either grown by sowing seed where it is to grow, a less labour intensive but less regular way of planting, or by initially growing the rice in small nursery fields, where it can be nurtured, and then transplanting it to larger fields. Paddy fields, which are sunken, with raised dams around them, are irrigated with water channels. The channels are filled by rainfall supplied by Thailand's monsoonal climate. Rice is harvested, dried and husked by the farmer or village collective, or taken to a rice mill to be sold as raw rice.

Paddy fields are a common sight in Thailand where farmers help each other with planting and harvesting by growing crops in rotation.

VEGETABLES

# BABY EGGPLANT AND CHERRY TOMATO STIR-FRY

ALTHOUGH A MIXTURE OF THAI EGGPLANTS OF DIFFERENT COLOURS WILL MAKE THIS DISH MORE VISUALLY APPEALING, JUST ONE TYPE WILL DO FINE. THE EGGPLANTS MAY DISCOLOUR WHEN YOU COOK THEM BUT DON'T WORRY AS THE FLAVOUR WON'T BE AFFECTED.

12 small round Thai eggplants
(aubergines), green, yellow
or purple
1 teaspoon fish sauce,
plus 1 tablespoon
1 tablespoon vegetable oil
1 small red chilli, chopped
1 tablespoon finely sliced ginger
2 Asian shallots, finely chopped
1 garlic clove, chopped
150 g (5 oz) cherry tomatoes
2 tablespoons black vinegar
2 tablespoons palm sugar
12–18 Thai sweet basil leaves

SERVES 4

CUT each eggplant in half and toss them in a bowl with 1 teaspoon fish sauce. Put about 8 cm (3 inches) of water in a wok and bring to the boil. Place the eggplants in a bamboo steamer, place the steamer over the boiling water and steam the eggplants for 15 minutes.

HEAT the oil in a wok, add the chilli, ginger, shallots and garlic and cook for 15 seconds. Add the eggplants and tomatoes and toss well. Add the black vinegar, sugar and remaining fish sauce and cook for 2 to 3 minutes, until the sauce thickens. Stir in the basil leaves and serve.

STIR-FRIED BROCCOLI WITH OYSTER SAUCE

# STIR-FRIED BROCCOLI WITH OYSTER SAUCE

350 g (12 oz) Chinese broccoli,
cut into pieces
1 tablespoon vegetable oil
2 garlic cloves, finely chopped
1 tablespoon oyster sauce
1 tablespoon light soy sauce

SERVES 4

BLANCH the Chinese broccoli in boiling salted water for 2 to 3 minutes, then drain thoroughly.

HEAT the oil in a wok or frying pan and stir-fry the garlic over a medium heat until light brown. Add the Chinese broccoli and half of the oyster sauce and the light soy sauce. Stir-fry over a high heat for 1 to 2 minutes until the stems are just tender. Drizzle with the remaining oyster sauce.

## YAM TUA PHUU
# WING BEAN SALAD

THIS IS A FRESH, CRUNCHY SALAD THAT LOOKS GOOD ON THE TABLE. WING BEANS HAVE FOUR
FRILLY EDGES TO THEM AND AN INTERESTING CROSS SECTION WHEN CUT.

oil, for frying
75 g (3 oz) Asian shallots,
    finely sliced
175 g (6 oz) wing beans
55 g (2 oz) cooked chicken, shredded
1 lemon grass stalk, white part only,
    finely sliced
2 tablespoons dried shrimp, ground
1½ tablespoons fish sauce
3–4 tablespoons lime juice
½ long red chilli or 1 small red chilli,
    finely chopped
55 g (2 oz) whole salted roasted
    peanuts
125 ml (½ cup) coconut milk
    (page 279), for garnish

SERVES 4

HEAT 2.5 cm (1 inch) oil in a wok or deep frying
pan over a medium heat. Deep-fry the shallots for
3 to 4 minutes until they are light brown (without
burning them). Lift out with a slotted spoon and
drain on paper towels.

SLICE the wing beans diagonally into thin pieces.
Blanch the wing beans in boiling water for
30 seconds, then drain and put them in cold
water for 1 to 2 minutes. Drain and transfer to a
bowl. Add the cooked chicken, lemon grass,
dried shrimp, fish sauce, lime juice, chilli and
half the peanuts. Mix with a spoon. Taste, then
adjust the seasoning if necessary.

PUT the wing bean salad in a serving bowl, drizzle
with coconut milk and sprinkle with the crispy
shallots and the rest of the peanuts.

## PHAT PHAK BUNG
# STIR-FRIED WATER SPINACH

THE VEGETABLE THAT THE CHINESE CALL 'ONG CHOY' IS POPULAR IN THAILAND WHERE IT'S CALLED
'PHAK BUNG'. IT HAS LONG THIN STALKS AND LEAFY TOPS, ALL OF WHICH ARE GOOD TO EAT. BUY IT
FROM ASIAN SUPERMARKETS WHERE IT IS SOMETIMES CALLED MORNING GLORY.

1½ tablespoons oyster sauce
1 teaspoon fish sauce
1 tablespoon yellow bean sauce
¼ teaspoon sugar
1½ tablespoons vegetable oil
2–3 garlic cloves, finely chopped
350 g (12 oz) water spinach, cut
    into 5 cm (2 inch) lengths
1 red bird's eye chilli, slightly
    crushed (optional)

SERVES 4

MIX the oyster sauce, fish sauce, yellow bean
sauce and sugar in a small bowl.

HEAT the oil in a wok or a frying pan and stir-fry
the garlic over a medium heat until light brown.
Increase the heat to very high, add the stalks
of the water spinach and stir-fry for 1 to 2 minutes.
Add the leaves of the water spinach, the sauce
mixture and the crushed chilli and stir-fry for
another minute.

STIR-FRIED WATER SPINACH

PUMPKIN WITH CHILLI AND
BASIL

PHAT THUA FAK YAO

# STIR-FRIED SNAKE BEANS

SNAKE BEANS ARE VERY LONG GREEN BEANS AND ARE USUALLY SOLD IN COILS. YOU CAN LEAVE OUT
THE CHICKEN IF YOU PREFER, BUT REMEMBER THAT THIS STILL WON'T BE A VEGETARIAN DISH AS IT
CONTAINS RED CURRY PASTE, WHICH HAS FISH SAUCE AND SHRIMP PASTE IN IT.

2 tablespoons vegetable oil
2 teaspoons red curry paste
   (page 276) or bought paste
350 g (12 oz) skinless chicken
   breast fillet, finely sliced
350 g (12 oz) snake beans,
   cut diagonally into 2.5 cm
   (1 inch) pieces
1 tablespoon fish sauce
25 g (1 oz) sugar
4 makrut (kaffir) lime leaves,
   very finely shredded

SERVES 4

HEAT the oil in a wok or frying pan and stir-fry the
red curry paste over a medium heat for 2 minutes
or until fragrant. Add the chicken and stir for 4 to
5 minutes or until the chicken is cooked. Add the
beans, fish sauce and sugar. Stir-fry for another
4 to 5 minutes.

TRANSFER to a serving plate and sprinkle with the
makrut lime leaves.

PHAT FAK THAWNG KUB PHRIK

# PUMPKIN WITH CHILLI AND BASIL

3 tablespoons dried shrimp
½ teaspoon shrimp paste
2 coriander (cilantro) roots
10–12 white peppercorns
2 garlic cloves, chopped
2 Asian shallots, chopped
125 ml (½ cup) coconut cream
   (page 279)
300 g (10 oz) butternut pumpkin
   (squash), cut into 4 cm (1½ inch)
   cubes
2 large red chillies, cut lengthways
125 ml (½ cup) coconut milk
   (page 279)
1 tablespoon fish sauce
1 tablespoon palm sugar
2 teaspoons lime juice
12 Thai sweet basil leaves

SERVES 4

SOAK 2 tablespoons of the dried shrimp in a small
bowl of water for 20 minutes, then drain.

PUT the remaining dried shrimp, shrimp paste,
coriander roots, peppercorns, garlic and shallots in
a pestle and mortar or food processor and pound
or blend to a paste.

BRING the coconut cream to a boil in a saucepan
and simmer for 5 minutes. Add the paste and stir
to combine. Cook for another 2 to 3 minutes, then
add the pumpkin, chillies, rehydrated shrimp and
coconut milk. Stir to combine all the ingredients and
simmer for 10 to 15 minutes, until the pumpkin is
just tender. Don't let the pumpkin turn to mush.

ADD the fish sauce, palm sugar and lime juice to
the pan and cook for another 2 to 3 minutes. Stir
in the basil leaves before serving.

PHAT PAK RUAM

# STIR-FRIED MIXED VEGETABLES

CARROTS, SNOW PEAS AND ASPARAGUS ARE NOT TYPICALLY THAI BUT THEY ARE NOW WIDELY GROWN AND EATEN. THE NORTH-WEST OF THAILAND HAS THE RIGHT CLIMATE FOR GROWING COLDER WEATHER VEGETABLES, PARTICULARLY PLACES LIKE THE KING'S PROJECT NORTH OF CHIANG MAI.

4 thin asparagus spears
4 baby sweet corn
50 g (2 oz) snake beans
110 g (4 oz) mixed red and yellow
    capsicums (peppers)
½ small carrot
50 g (2 oz) Chinese broccoli or
    broccoli florets
25 g (1 oz) snow peas (mangetout),
    topped and tailed
2 cm (¾ inch) piece of ginger,
    finely sliced
1 tablespoon fish sauce
1½ tablespoons oyster sauce
2 tablespoons vegetable stock
    or water
½ teaspoon sugar
1½ tablespoons vegetable oil
3–4 garlic cloves, finely chopped
2 spring onions (scallions), sliced

SERVES 4

CUT off the tips of the asparagus and slice each spear into 5 cm (2 inch) lengths. Cut the sweet corn in halves lengthways and the beans into 2.5 cm (1 inch) lengths. Cut both on an angle. Halve the capsicums and remove the seeds, then cut into bite-sized pieces. Peel the carrot and cut into batons.

BLANCH the asparagus stalks, sweet corn, beans and broccoli florets in boiling salted water for 30 seconds. Remove and place in a bowl of iced water to ensure a crispy texture. Drain and place in a bowl with the capsicum, carrot, snow peas, asparagus tips and ginger.

MIX the fish sauce, oyster sauce, stock and sugar in a small bowl.

HEAT the oil in a wok or frying pan and stir-fry the garlic over a medium heat until light brown. Add the mixed vegetables and the sauce mixture, then stir-fry over a high heat for 2 to 3 minutes. Taste, then adjust the seasoning if necessary. Add the spring onions and toss.

Vegetables for stir-fries should be cut into a uniform size.

# SPICY TOMATO DIPPING SAUCE

THIS FAMOUS DIPPING SAUCE FROM CHIANG MAI SHOULD BE SERVED AS A MAIN COURSE WITH BLANCHED VEGETABLES SUCH AS WEDGES OF EGGPLANT OR CABBAGE, PIECES OF SNAKE BEAN OR PUMPKIN, AND ASPARAGUS SPEARS. PIECES OF DEEP-FRIED PORK SKIN ARE ALSO SUITABLE.

1 dried long red chilli
1 lemon grass stalk, white part only,
    finely sliced
4 Asian shallots, finely chopped
2–3 garlic cloves, roughly chopped
½ teaspoon shrimp paste
1½ tablespoons vegetable oil
175 g (6 oz) minced (ground) fatty
    pork
450 g (1 lb) tomatoes,
    finely chopped
2 tablespoons fish sauce
1 tablespoon sugar
3 tablespoons tamarind purée
mixed vegetables, such as wedges
    of eggplant (aubergine), pieces of
    snake bean, wedges of cabbage,
    asparagus spears, baby corn,
    pieces of pumpkin, to serve
a few coriander (cilantro) leaves,
    for garnish
pieces of pork skin, deep-fried,
    to serve

SERVES 4

SLIT the chilli lengthways with a sharp knife and discard all the seeds. Soak the chilli in hot water for 1 to 2 minutes or until soft, then drain and chop roughly. Using a pestle and mortar, pound the chilli, lemon grass, shallots and garlic into a paste. Add the shrimp paste and mix well. Alternatively, use a small processor or blender to grind or blend the chilli, lemon grass, shallots, garlic and shrimp paste into a smooth paste.

HEAT the oil in a saucepan or wok and stir-fry the paste over a medium heat for 2 minutes or until fragrant. Add the minced pork and stir for 2 to 3 minutes. Add the tomatoes, fish sauce, sugar and tamarind. Reduce the heat and gently simmer for 25 to 30 minutes or until the mixture is thick.

BLANCH briefly any tough vegetables such as eggplant, snake beans, asparagus and pumpkin. Drain well.

TASTE the sauce, then adjust with more tamarind, sugar or chilli if necessary. This dish should have three flavours: sweet, sour and lightly salted. Spoon into a serving bowl and garnish with coriander leaves. Serve with a mixture of blanched vegetables and deep-fried pork skin.

## NAAM PHRIK KA-PI
# SHRIMP PASTE DIPPING SAUCE

THAI HOT DIPPING SAUCE IS USED TO ACCOMPANY GRILLED OR DEEP-FRIED FISH, PIECES OF OMELETTE, AND FRESH VEGETABLES AND FRUIT SUCH AS EGGPLANT, CUCUMBER, WING BEANS AND SNAKE BEANS. YOU CAN VARY THE NUMBER OF CHILLIES, DEPENDING ON HOW HOT YOU LIKE IT.

3–4 garlic cloves
2 teaspoons shrimp paste
2–3 small red and green chillies
3–4 Thai eggplants (aubergines) (optional)
1 teaspoon sugar
1 tablespoon fish sauce
2 tablespoons lime juice
mixed raw vegetables and fruit such as pieces of Thai eggplant (aubergine), cucumber batons, wing beans, pieces of snake bean, spring onions (scallions), pomelo segments, pieces of rose apple, to serve

SERVES 4

USING a pestle and mortar, pound the garlic into a rough paste. Add the shrimp paste and grind together. Add the chillies and lightly bruise to release the hot taste. (Do this gently so the liquid won't splash.) Add the eggplants and lightly pound. Add the sugar, fish sauce and lime juice and lightly mix in. Taste the sauce, then adjust the seasoning if necessary.

TO MAKE without a pestle and mortar, put the finely chopped garlic in a bowl and, using the back of a spoon, scrape the garlic into a paste. Add the shrimp paste and mix well. Add the chillies and break them up with a fork. Add the eggplant and squash it gently against the side of the bowl. Add the sugar, fish sauce and lime juice and lightly mix.

SPOON into a small serving bowl and serve with the mixed vegetables.

When you have pounded the ingredients together, stir in the sugar, fish sauce and lime juice.

# DESSERTS

KHAO NIAW MAMUANG

## STICKY RICE WITH MANGO

IN THAILAND THE MANGO SEASON IS IN APRIL. SOME MANGOES TASTE BETTER WHEN GREEN, CRISP AND CRUNCHY, OTHERS WHEN THEY ARE RIPE. EITHER WAY, THERE IS A LOT OF VARIETY AND MANY DIFFERENT FLAVOURS. THIS STICKY RICE WITH MANGO IS ARGUABLY THE BEST THAI DESSERT.

4 large ripe mangoes
1 quantity of steamed sticky rice
   with coconut milk (page 280)
170 ml (⅔ cup) coconut cream
   (page 279) mixed with ¼ teaspoon
   salt, for garnish
2 tablespoons dry-fried mung beans
   (optional)

SERVES 4

PEEL the mangoes and slice off the two outside cheeks of each, removing as much flesh as you can in large pieces. Avoid cutting very close to the stone where the flesh is fibrous. Discard the stone. Slice each cheek lengthways into four or five pieces.

ARRANGE the mango pieces on a serving plate. Spoon a portion of steamed sticky rice with coconut milk near the mango slices. Spoon the coconut cream garnish on top and sprinkle with mung beans. Serve at room temperature.

BANANA IN COCONUT CREAM

KLUAY BUAT CHII

## BANANA IN COCONUT CREAM

THERE ARE MORE THAN 20 VARIETIES OF BANANA IN THAILAND, ALL OF WHICH ARE USED IN COOKING. USE NICE SWEET BANANAS FOR THIS RECIPE AND AVOID PARTICULARLY LARGE ONES.

400 ml (1⅔ cups) coconut milk
   (page 279)
4 tablespoons sugar
5 just-ripe bananas
½ teaspoon salt

SERVES 4

PUT the coconut milk, sugar and 125 ml (½ cup) water in a saucepan and bring to a boil. Reduce the heat and simmer until the sugar dissolves.

PEEL the bananas and cut them into 5 cm (2 inch) lengths. If you are using very small bananas, leave them whole.

WHEN the sugar in the coconut milk has dissolved, add the bananas and salt. Cook gently over a low to medium heat for 5 minutes or until the bananas are soft.

DIVIDE the bananas and coconut cream among four bowls. Serve warm or at room temperature.

SAKU PEAK KAB MA PRAO ON

# TAPIOCA PUDDING WITH YOUNG COCONUT

170 ml (⅔ cup) coconut milk
  (page 279)
¾ teaspoon salt
110 g (4 oz) tapioca or sago
6 pandanus leaves
60 g (¼ cup) caster (superfine) sugar
150 g (5 oz) young coconut meat in
  syrup (from a tin), drained

SERVES 4

IN a small saucepan, stir the coconut milk with ½ teaspoon salt until combined.

BRING 1 litre (4 cups) water to a rolling boil in a medium saucepan. Add the tapioca and pandanus leaves and stir occasionally with a wooden spoon for 15 to 20 minutes while simmering over a medium heat. Stir until all the grains are swollen, clear and shiny. Reduce the heat if necessary. Add the sugar and ¼ teaspoon salt to the saucepan and stir until the sugar has dissolved. The tapioca should now be almost cooked. Add the coconut meat and gently mix. Remove the pandanus leaves. Leave to thicken for 5 minutes before dividing among individual bowls. Drizzle coconut milk on top. Serve warm.

Stir the tapioca and pandanus leaves occasionally.

KLUAY THAWT

# DEEP-FRIED BANANAS

YEARS AGO MOST THAI PEOPLE WERE BROUGHT UP ON THIS DELICIOUS SNACK BUT IT IS NOT AS EASY TODAY TO FIND IT ON THE STREET. HOWEVER, YOU CAN EASILY MAKE IT AT HOME, JUST AS MANY THAI PEOPLE DO. ANOTHER VERSION USES SWEET POTATOES WITH THE BANANAS.

DEEP-FRIED BANANAS

BATTER
125 g (1 cup) self-raising flour
½ teaspoon baking powder
2 teaspoons sugar
¼ teaspoon salt
25 g (1 oz) grated coconut
  (page 279) or desiccated coconut
2 tablespoons sesame seeds
350 ml (1⅜ cups) water, at room
  temperature

vegetable oil, for deep-frying
4 ripe bananas

SERVES 4

PUT the flour, baking powder, sugar, salt, coconut and sesame seeds in a bowl. Add the water and lightly mix with a spoon or fork until smooth.

HEAT 7.5 cm (3 inches) oil in a wok or deep-frying pan over a medium heat. When the oil seems hot, drop a little batter into the oil. If it sizzles immediately, the oil is ready. It is important not to have the oil too hot or the batter will burn.

HALVE the bananas lengthways, then cut them into 5 cm (2 inch) chunks. Preheat the oven to 150°C/300°F/Gas 2. Dip the banana chunks one at a time into the batter, then lower into the hot oil. Deep-fry about 5 pieces at a time for 3 to 4 minutes or until golden, then lift out with a slotted spoon or a pair of chopsticks. Drain on paper towels and keep warm in the oven. Transfer to a serving plate and serve warm.

When you have coloured and floured the water chestnuts, cook them in two batches. When they float, lift them out.

Detail from a Wat in Ratchaburi.

## THAPTHIM KRAWP
# CRISP RUBIES

CRISP RUBIES RESEMBLE JEWEL-LIKE PIECES OF POMEGRANATE. THE COMBINATION OF INGREDIENTS MAY SOUND SOMEWHAT ODD, BUT CRISP RUBIES ARE VERY POPULAR AND ARE ACTUALLY QUITE DELICIOUS, ESPECIALLY WHEN SERVED WITH ICE AND COCONUT CREAM.

8–10 drops of pink or red food colouring
2 x 225 g (8 oz) tins water chestnuts, drained and each chestnut cut into 10–12 pieces
150 g (5 oz) tapioca flour
250 g (1 cup) sugar
185 ml (¾ cup) coconut milk (page 279)
¼ teaspoon salt
crushed ice, to serve

SERVES 6

ADD the food colouring to 60 ml (¼ cup) water in a bowl. Add the water chestnuts and mix with a spoon. Leave for 10 minutes until the pieces turn pink, then drain and leave to dry.

PUT the tapioca flour in a plastic bag. Add the pink water chestnuts and shake the bag to coat them well. Dust off any excess flour. Bring a saucepan of water to boiling point. Add half of the water chestnuts and cook for 1 to 2 minutes or until they float to the surface. Lift out with a slotted spoon and put them in a bowl of cold water. Repeat with the remaining water chestnuts. Drain all the pieces.

IN a small saucepan, heat 250 ml (1 cup) water and the sugar until the mixture boils, stirring constantly. Lower the heat to medium and simmer for 5 to 10 minutes until the liquid reduces to a thick syrup.

MIX the coconut milk and salt in a small saucepan and cook over a medium heat for 1 to 2 minutes until slightly creamy.

DIVIDE the water chestnuts among individual bowls and top with a few spoonfuls each of sugar syrup and creamy coconut milk. Sprinkle with ice and serve cold.

KHAO NIAW DAM

# BLACK STICKY RICE WITH TARO

VEGETABLES LIKE TARO ARE OFTEN USED IN THAI DESSERTS. BLACK STICKY RICE IS SIMPLY WHITE RICE WITH THE BRAN LEFT ON AND IS ACTUALLY MORE PURPLE THAN BLACK. YOU MUST COOK THE RICE BEFORE ADDING ANY SUGAR OR IT WILL TOUGHEN AND NEVER BECOME TENDER.

175 g (6 oz) black sticky rice
  (black glutinous)
280 g (10 oz) taro, cut into 1 cm
  (½ inch) squares and soaked in
  cold water
150 g (5 oz) palm sugar
1 teaspoon salt
185 ml (¾ cup) coconut milk
  (page 279)

SERVES 6

PUT the rice in a bowl and pour in cold water to come 5 cm (2 inches) above the rice. Soak for at least 3 hours, or overnight if possible.

DRAIN the rice and add clean water. Scoop the rice through your fingers four or five times to clean it, then drain. Repeat two or three times with clean water to remove the unwanted starch. (The water will never be completely clear when using black rice, even when all the unwanted starch has gone.) Put the rice in a saucepan and add 625 ml (2½ cups) cold water.

BRING to the boil, stirring the rice frequently as it reaches boiling point. Reduce the heat to medium. Stir and simmer for 30 to 35 minutes or until nearly all the liquid has been absorbed. The rice should be very moist, but with hardly any water remaining in the bottom of the saucepan. (Taste a few grains to check whether the rice is cooked.)

MEANWHILE, drain the taro, spread it on a plate and transfer it to a bamboo steamer or other steamer. Taking care not to burn your hands, set the basket over a pan of boiling water over a high heat. Cover and steam for 8 to 10 minutes or until the taro is cooked and tender.

WHEN the rice is cooked, add the sugar and gently stir until the sugar has dissolved. Add the taro and gently mix.

MIX the salt into the coconut milk. Divide the pudding among individual bowls and drizzle coconut milk on top. Serve warm.

Black sticky rice is commonly used for desserts and, when cooked, is actually a dark purplish-red.

Akah bracelets for sale.

Cut off the tops of the pumpkins
and scrape out the seeds. Sieve
the custard, discard the leaves,
then pour into the pumpkins.

# PUMPKIN WITH CUSTARD

THIS TRADITIONAL THAI DESSERT, MADE WITH COCONUT MILK AND PALM OR COCONUT SUGAR, IS
SWEET AND RICH IN TASTE. CHOOSE HONEY-COLOURED PUMPKINS, EITHER ONE SMALL TO MEDIUM,
OR FOUR VERY SMALL ONES. WHEN COOKED AND COOLED, CUT THEM INTO WEDGES FOR SERVING.

2 tablespoons coconut milk
  (page 279)
2 eggs
150 g (5 oz) palm sugar, cut or
  shaved into very small pieces
2–3 pandanus leaves, dried
  and cut into small pieces,
  and bruised, or 1 teaspoon
  vanilla essence
1 small to medium or 4 very small
  pumpkins

SERVES 4

TO make a custard, stir the coconut milk, eggs,
palm sugar, pandanus leaves and a pinch of salt in
a bowl, using a spoon, for 10 minutes or until the
sugar has dissolved.

POUR the custard through a sieve into a jug to
discard the pandanus leaves. Pour the custard
into the pumpkin/s, filling to within 2.5 cm (1 inch)
from the top.

CAREFULLY cut off the top of the pumpkin/s. Try
not to pierce the pumpkin at any other point with
the knife as it is more likely to crack or leak around
such punctures. Using a spoon, scrape out and
discard all the seeds and fibres.

FILL a wok or a steamer pan with water, cover and
bring to a rolling boil over a high heat. Place the
pumpkin/s on a plate. Use a plate that will fit on
the rack of a traditional bamboo steamer basket or
on a steamer rack inside the wok. Taking care not
to burn your hands, place the plate on the rack or
steamer inside the wok. Cover, reduce the heat to
low and cook for 30 to 45 minutes or until the
pumpkin is cooked and the custard puffed up.
Check and replenish the water every 10 minutes
or so.

TURN off the heat and remove the cover. Carefully
remove the pumpkin and set aside to cool. If you
prefer, you can leave the pumpkin in the steamer
to cool to room temperature.

CUT the pumpkin into thick wedges for serving.
Serve at room temperature or chilled.

AS an alternative, you can steam the mixture in a
shallow tin, such as a pie tin or cake pan, and
serve it in small spoonfuls on top of mounds of
steamed sticky rice with coconut milk (page 280).

## SANGKAYA
# CUSTARDS

THE CLASSIC CUSTARD COOKED IN A PUMPKIN IS JUST ONE OF MANY POPULAR CUSTARDS IN THAILAND. AS HERE, COCONUT, SWEET POTATO, JACKFRUIT AND TARO ARE ALSO USED AS FLAVOURINGS. SERVE IN BANANA CUPS, AS SHOWN, OR POUR THE MIXTURE INTO BABY PUMPKINS.

Make and balance the cups carefully so none of the liquid spills out.

banana leaves
80 ml (⅓ cup) coconut milk
  (page 279)
7 eggs
275 g (10 oz) palm sugar, cut into
  very small pieces
¼ teaspoon salt
5–6 fresh pandanus leaves, dried
  and cut into small pieces, bruised,
  or 3 teaspoons vanilla essence
100 g (3 oz) young coconut meat,
  cut into small pieces, or orange
  sweet potato, jackfruit or taro,
  cut into matchsticks

MAKES 6

TO SOFTEN the banana leaves and prevent them from splitting, put them in a hot oven for about 10 seconds, or blanch them briefly. Cut the banana leaves into 12 circles about 13 cm (5 inches) in diameter with the fibre running lengthways. Place one piece with the fibre running lengthways and another on top of it with the fibre running across. Make a 1 cm (½ inches) tuck 4 cm (1½ inch) long (4 cm in from the edge and no further) and pin securely with a small sharp toothpick. Repeat this at the opposite point and at the two side points, making four tucks altogether. Flatten the base as best you can. Repeat to make 6 square-shaped cups. Alternatively, use a small shallow rectangular tin such as a brownie tin.

COMBINE the coconut milk, eggs, sugar, salt and pandanus leaves in a bowl, using a spoon, for 10 minutes or until the sugar has dissolved. Pour the custard through the sieve into a bowl to discard the pandanus leaves.

ADD the coconut, orange sweet potato, taro or jackfruit to the custard and lightly mix. Spoon the mixture into each banana cup, filling to within 1 cm (½ inch) from the top.

HALF FILL a wok or a steamer pan with water, cover and bring to a rolling boil over a high heat. Place the banana cups on a plate. Use a plate that will fit on the rack of a traditional bamboo steamer basket or on a steamer rack inside the wok or pan. Taking care not to burn your hands, place the plate on the bamboo steamer or steamer rack inside the wok or pan. Cover, reduce the heat to low and cook for 10 to 15 minutes. Check and replenish the water after 10 minutes. Serve at room temperature or chilled. The custards can be covered and refrigerated for up to 3 to 4 days.

Preparing durian for sale.

ICE CREAM KRA TI
# COCONUT ICE CREAM

400 ml (1⅔ cups) coconut milk
   (page 279)
250 ml (1 cup) thick (double/heavy)
   cream
2 eggs
4 egg yolks
160 g (⅔ cup) caster (superfine)
   sugar
¼ teaspoon salt

SERVES 10

POUR the coconut milk and cream into a medium saucepan. Stir over a gentle heat without boiling for 2 to 3 minutes. Remove from the heat, cover and keep warm over a bowl of boiling water.

PUT the eggs, egg yolks, sugar and salt in a large heatproof bowl. Beat the mixture with electric beaters for 3 minutes or until frothy and thickened.

PLACE the bowl over a pan of simmering water. Continue to beat the egg mixture, slowly adding all the coconut mixture until the custard thickens lightly. This process will take 8 to 10 minutes. The mixture should be a thin cream and easily coat the back of a spoon. Do not boil it or it will curdle. Set aside until cool. Stir the mixture occasionally while it is cooling. Pour into a freezer box or churn in an ice cream machine. If you are using a freezer box, take the mixture out of the freezer and beat it with electric beaters at least twice during the freezing. You want it to get plenty of air whipped into it. Cover and freeze completely. To serve, remove from the freezer for 10 to 15 minutes until slightly softened. Serve in scoops with slices of coconut.

ICE CREAM MAMUANG
# MANGO SORBET

3 ripe mangoes
150 g (5½ oz) palm sugar
zest and juice from 1 lime

SERVES 4

PEEL the mangoes and cut the flesh off the stones. Chop into small pieces. Put the sugar and 185 ml (¾ cup) water in a saucepan and bring to the boil. Reduce the heat and simmer until the liquid reduces by half. Put the sugar syrup, mango and lime zest and juice in a food processor or blender and whiz until smooth.

POUR into a freezer box or churn in an ice cream machine. If you are using a freezer box, take the mixture out of the freezer and beat it with electric beaters at least twice during the freezing time. You want it to have plenty of air whipped into it or it will be too icy and hard. Cover and freeze completely.

MANGO SORBET

PALMS Phetchaburi province is famous for its sweets. It is also the land of the palm tree. Both coconut and sugar palms supply the sweet-makers with raw ingredients to ply their trade. Coconut is used both fresh and dried. When fresh, the flesh is soft and jelly-like with lots of liquid inside and these coconuts are sold for drinking (left). Older, drier coconut flesh, however, is shredded (bottom centre) and used as a garnish.

# SWEETS

PEOPLE IN THAILAND USE THE TERM KHWANG WAAN, LITERALLY MEANING SWEET STUFF, TO REFER TO ANYTHING THAT IS SWEET, INCLUDING DESSERTS, SWEET SNACKS OR SWEETS THEMSELVES. MOST KHWANG WAAN ARE EATEN AS SNACKS RATHER THAN AS DESSERTS BUT NEVERTHELESS MEALS CAN BE FINISHED ON A SWEET NOTE.

In Thailand sweet things have always been part of the cuisine, originally made with crushed beans, coconut, rice, sugar and fruit. These were supplemented with the use of eggs and pastry, ideas that arrived with the Portuguese. Even more recently, ice cream has become popular.

## TEXTURES, COLOURS AND FLAVOURS
Thai sweets differ from European ones in both texture and flavour. Though egg custards and pastries may be reminiscent of European desserts, they are often much sweeter. Unlike in Europe, salt is used as a flavour in coconut desserts and sweets, to offset sweetness. Flower and leaf perfumes such as jasmine and pandanus are used in sugar syrups. Favourite textures include jellies, custards and sticky,

Coconut is used to flavour sticky rice, which is steamed in leaves (opposite page bottom right and this page bottom left). Palm sugar comes in different grades, the best being from Phetchaburi province. It is usually sold in discs or log shapes (bottom centre) though softer types can come in tubs. Palm sugar is used to sweeten Thai style waffles (top) and used in perfumed syrups for 'wet' sweets and layered sweets (right).

chewy ingredients like rice. Often combinations of textures are eaten together, particularly in desserts like 'green strings' where 'strings' made of green dough are served with crushed ice, sugar syrup and coconut juice. Colours come from pandanus (green), egg yolks (yellow), and coconut ash and sesame (black). Crunch is often added by adding lotus seeds, beans, sweet corn kernels and water chestnuts. Fruit is eaten fresh and is also candied and preserved.

## FESTIVALS

Some sweets are associated with ceremonies and in many cases are thought to sweeten the gods. Other sweets are eaten at particular times of the year, ash pudding at Thai New Year, and sticky rice with banana at the end of Thai Lent.

## CUSTARDS

**COCONUT CUSTARDS** *(sangkaya)* These popular baked coconut custards are made with duck eggs, palm sugar and coconut milk at the Mei Kim Lui sweet factory. Hundreds of custards are made every morning and sent out to the shops owned by the factory. The ingredients are all local to Phetchaburi, a province famous for its palm sugar. The cook mixes the custard in large quantities and pours it into small tin

containers set out on baking sheets. The custards are baked in an oven for about an hour before being cooled. They are then sold in their containers. Some custards have different toppings: sliced garlic, shallots or peanuts are particularly popular. The use of egg to make custard-type sweets is probably based on Portuguese desserts introduced in the 14th and 15th centuries.

## PALM SUGAR

**PALM SUGAR** Palm sugar is made by boiling the sap of sugar palms *(ton taan)*. The sap is collected twice a day, in the early morning and early evening. It is then boiled until it reaches the desired thickness. Pandanus leaves are used to flavour some syrups, others are left plain. The thinnest syrup is sold in bottles to be sold as juice, which is drunk poured over ice. The thickest crystallizes to a solid sugar.

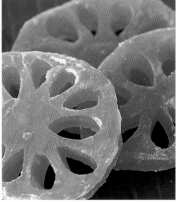

CANDIED LOTUS ROOT
Candied fruit and vegetables are popular sweets. Slices of lotus root are simmered in a sugar syrup until they candy.

GOLDEN FLOWERS These are made by piping duck egg yolks into simmering sugar syrup to form golden flowers. Here they are piled into little pastry cups.

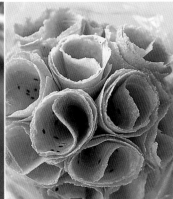

PALM FRUIT IN SUGAR SYRUP Palm fruit in sugar syrup is sold by the scoop in small plastic bags. Coconut milk is added as a garnish.

BEAN PASTE SWEETS Thick sweetened mung bean paste is moulded into a variety of different attractive fruit shapes. Here they resemble mangosteens.

COCONUT PUDDINGS These puddings have a transparent sweet jelly with chestnut or lotus seeds on the bottom and a salty coconut jelly on top.

COCONUT CUSTARDS (sangkaya fak thawang) These are a common sweet snack. Coconut custard is steamed in small hollowed out pumpkins.

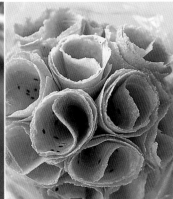

COCONUT WAFERS These thin, crisp coconut wafers are made with coconut, rice flour and palm sugar. Rolled into cones and packed in cellophane.

CHINESE CAKES These Chinese-style pastry cakes are filled with green mung beans or red beans. Often given as gifts at weddings and birthdays.

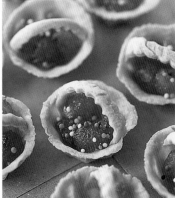

PASTRY CUPS This is a modern Thai sweet made by filling a pastry cup with a dark sweet palm sugar mixture. Hundreds and thousands add colour.

DIPPED FRUITS (luuk chup) These are the most intricate Thai sweets. Made from soy bean paste and dipped into a clear jelly that dries to a waxy glaze.

JELLIES These jellies are made with durian (brown), pandanus leaves (green) and sesame (black). Each jelly is wrapped in a piece of cellophane.

BLACK STICKY RICE This is a popular dessert made with a sticky rice that is purple rather than black. Sold in little bags with some salted coconut cream.

# BASICS &
# ACCOMPANIMENTS

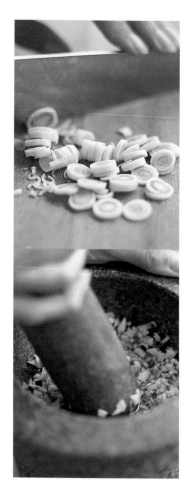

Pound the chopped ingredients until a smooth paste is formed.

CHIANG MAI CURRY PASTE

## KHREUANG KAENG PHANAENG
# DRY CURRY PASTE

2 dried long red chillies, about
    13 cm (5 inches) long
2 lemon grass stalks, white part
    only, finely sliced
2.5 cm (1 inch) piece of galangal,
    finely chopped
4–5 garlic cloves, finely chopped
3–4 Asian shallots, finely chopped
5–6 coriander (cilantro) roots,
    finely chopped
1 teaspoon shrimp paste
1 teaspoon ground cumin,
    dry-roasted
3 tablespoons unsalted peanuts,
    chopped

MAKES 80 G (⅓ CUP)

REMOVE the stems from the chillies and slit the chillies lengthways with a sharp knife. Discard the seeds and soak the chillies in hot water for 1 to 2 minutes or until soft. Drain and roughly chop.

USING a pestle and mortar, pound the chillies, lemon grass and galangal into a paste. Add the remaining ingredients one at a time and pound until the mixture forms a very smooth paste.

ALTERNATIVELY, you can use a food processor or blender to blend all the ingredients together into as smooth a paste as possible. Add cooking oil, as needed, to assist the blending.

USE as required or keep in an airtight jar. The paste will keep for at least two weeks in the refrigerator and for two months in a freezer.

## KHREUANG KAENG HANGLEH
# CHIANG MAI CURRY PASTE

1 tablespoon coriander seeds
2 teaspoons cumin seeds
2 dried long red chillies, about
    13 cm (5 inches) long
½ teaspoon salt
5 cm (2 inch) piece of galangal,
    grated
1 lemon grass stalk, white part only,
    finely chopped
2 Asian shallots, chopped
2 garlic cloves, chopped
1 teaspoon grated turmeric or
    a pinch of ground turmeric
1 teaspoon shrimp paste
½ teaspoon ground cassia
    or cinnamon

MAKES 185 G (¾ CUP)

DRY-ROAST the coriander seeds in a small frying pan for 1 minute until fragrant, then remove from the pan. Repeat with the cumin seeds. Grind them both to a powder with a pestle and mortar.

REMOVE the stems from the chillies and slit the chillies lengthways with a sharp knife. Discard the seeds. Soak the chillies in hot water for 1 to 2 minutes or until soft. Drain and roughly chop.

USING a pestle and mortar, pound the chillies, salt, galangal, lemon grass, shallots, garlic and turmeric to as smooth a paste as possible. Add the shrimp paste, ground coriander, cumin and cassia and mix until the mixture forms a smooth paste.

ALTERNATIVELY, use a small processor or blender to blend all the ingredients into a very smooth paste. Add a little cooking oil, as needed, to ease the grinding.

## KHREUANG KAENG KHIAW-WAAN
# GREEN CURRY PASTE

1 teaspoon ground coriander
1 teaspoon ground cumin
8–10 small green chillies, seeded
2 lemon grass stalks, white part
    only, finely sliced
2.5 cm (1 inch) piece of galangal,
    finely chopped
1 teaspoon very finely chopped
    makrut (kaffir) lime skin or makrut
    lime leaves (about half the skin
    from a makrut lime or 4–5 leaves)
4–5 garlic cloves, finely chopped
3–4 Asian shallots, chopped
5–6 coriander (cilantro) roots,
    finely chopped
a handful of holy basil leaves, finely
    chopped
2 teaspoons shrimp paste

MAKES 125 G (½ CUP)

DRY-ROAST the coriander in a small frying pan for 1 minute until fragrant, then remove from the pan. Repeat with the cumin.

USING a pestle and mortar, pound the chillies, lemon grass, galangal and makrut lime skin or leaves into a paste. Add the garlic, shallots and coriander roots and pound together. Add the remaining ingredients and dry-roasted spices one at a time and pound until the mixture forms a smooth paste.

ALTERNATIVELY, you can use a food processor or blender to blend all the ingredients into as smooth a paste as possible. Add cooking oil as needed to assist the blending.

USE as required or keep in an airtight jar. The paste will keep for at least two weeks in the refrigerator and for two months in a freezer.

Whether using makrut lime skin or leaves, chop them very finely. Dry-roasting the ground spices helps to bring out the flavour.

## KHREUANG KAENG LEUANG
# YELLOW CURRY PASTE

3 teaspoons coriander seeds,
    dry-roasted
1 teaspoon cumin seeds,
    dry-roasted
2–3 dried long red chillies
2 lemon grass stalks, white part
    only, finely sliced
3 Asian shallots, finely chopped
2 garlic cloves, finely chopped
2 tablespoons grated turmeric or
    1 teaspoon ground turmeric
1 teaspoon shrimp paste

MAKES 250 G (1 CUP)

GRIND the coriander seeds to a powder with a pestle and mortar. Grind the cumin seeds.

REMOVE the stems from the chillies and slit the chillies lengthways with a sharp knife. Discard the seeds and soak the chillies in hot water for 1 to 2 minutes or until soft. Drain and roughly chop.

USING a pestle and mortar, pound the chillies, lemon grass, shallots, garlic and turmeric to as smooth a paste as possible. Add the shrimp paste, ground coriander and ground cumin and pound until the mixture forms a smooth paste. Alternatively, use a small processor or blender, blend all the ingredients into a very smooth paste. Add cooking oil as needed to ease the grinding. Use as required or keep in an airtight jar. The paste will keep for at least two weeks in the refrigerator and for two months in a freezer.

YELLOW CURRY PASTE

Before soaking the dried chillies in hot water, slit them lengthways and remove all the seeds.

# RED CURRY PASTE

3–4 dried long red chillies, about
    13 cm (5 inches) long
8–10 dried small red chillies, about
    5 cm (2 inches) long, or 10 fresh
    small red chillies, seeded
2 lemon grass stalks, white part
    only, finely sliced
2.5 cm (1 inch) piece of galangal,
    finely sliced
1 teaspoon very finely chopped
    makrut (kaffir) lime skin or makrut
    lime leaves (about half the skin
    from a makrut lime or 4–5 leaves)
4–5 garlic cloves, finely chopped
3–4 Asian shallots, finely chopped
5–6 coriander (cilantro) roots,
    finely chopped
2 teaspoons shrimp paste
1 teaspoon ground coriander,
    dry-roasted

MAKES 125 G (½ CUP)

REMOVE the stems from the dried chillies and slit the chillies lengthways with a sharp knife. Discard the seeds and soak the chillies in hot water for 1 to 2 minutes or until soft. Drain and roughly chop.

USING a pestle and mortar, pound the chillies, lemon grass, galangal and makrut lime skin or leaves into a paste. Add the remaining ingredients and pound together until the mixture forms a smooth paste.

ALTERNATIVELY, you can use a food processor or blender to blend all the ingredients into as smooth a paste as possible. Add cooking oil, as needed, to assist the blending.

USE as required or keep in an airtight jar. The paste will keep for at least two weeks in the refrigerator and for two months in a freezer.

MASSAMAN CURRY PASTE

# MASSAMAN CURRY PASTE

2 dried long red chillies, about
    13 cm (5 inches) long
1 lemon grass stalk, white part only,
    finely sliced
2.5 cm (1 inch) piece of galangal,
    finely chopped
5 cloves
10 cm (4 inch) piece of cinnamon
    stick, crushed
10 cardamom seeds
½ teaspoon freshly grated nutmeg
6 garlic cloves, finely chopped
4 Asian shallots, finely chopped
4–5 coriander (cilantro) roots,
    finely chopped
1 teaspoon shrimp paste

MAKES 250 G (1 CUP)

REMOVE the stems from the chillies and slit the chillies lengthways with a sharp knife. Discard the seeds and soak the chillies in hot water for 1 to 2 minutes or until soft. Drain and roughly chop.

USING a pestle and mortar, pound the chillies, lemon grass, galangal, cloves, cinnamon, cardamom seeds and nutmeg into a paste. Add the garlic, shallots and coriander roots. Pound and mix together. Add the shrimp paste and pound until the mixture is a smooth paste.

ALTERNATIVELY, use a food processor or blender to grind or blend all the ingredients into as smooth a paste as possible. Add cooking oil, as needed, to assist the blending. Use as required or keep in an airtight jar. The paste will keep for two weeks in the refrigerator and for two months in a freezer.

KA-THI

# COCONUT MILK AND CREAM

GRATED COCONUT IS BEST WHEN IT IS FRESH. DRIED OR DESICCATED COCONUT CAN ALSO BE USED TO MAKE COCONUT MILK BUT IT NEEDS TO BE SOAKED, THEN CHOPPED MORE FINELY OR GROUND TO A PASTE, OTHERWISE IT WILL BE FIBROUS. IF YOU CAN, BUY A PROPER COCONUT GRATER.

1 coconut
  (yields about 300 g/10 oz flesh)

MAKES 125 ML (½ CUP) COCONUT CREAM AND 250 ML (1 CUP) COCONUT MILK

DRAIN the coconut by punching a hole in two of the dark, coloured eyes. Drain out the liquid and use it as a refreshing drink. Holding the coconut in one hand, tap around the circumference firmly with a hammer or pestle. This should cause the coconut to split open evenly. (If the coconut doesn't crack easily, put it in a 150°C/300°F/ Gas 2 oven for 15 minutes. This may cause it to crack as it cools. If it doesn't, it will crack easily when hit with a hammer.)

IF YOU would like to use a coconut grater, the easiest ones to use are the ones that you sit on at one end, then scrape out the coconut from each half on the serrated edge, catching the grated coconut meat in a large bowl. If you don't have a coconut grater, prise the flesh out of the shell, trim off the hard, brown, outer skin and grate either by hand on a box grater or chop in a food processor. Grated coconut can be frozen in small portions until it is needed.

MIX the grated coconut with 125 ml (½ cup) hot water and leave to steep for 5 minutes. Pour the mixture into a container through a sieve lined with muslin, then gather the muslin into a ball to squeeze out any remaining liquid. This will make a thick coconut milk, which is usually called coconut cream.

REPEAT the process with another 250 ml (1 cup) water to make thinner coconut milk.

Tap the coconut until it splits open. Pull it apart, scrape out the coconut and soak it in hot water before draining in a sieve.

STICKY RICE

STEAMED STICKY RICE WITH
COCONUT MILK

# STEAMED RICE

400 g (2 cups) jasmine rice

SERVES 4

RINSE the rice until the water runs clear. Put the rice in a saucepan and add enough water to come an index-finger joint above the rice. Bring to the boil, cover and cook at a slow simmer for 10 to 15 minutes. Remove from the heat and leave it to rest for 10 minutes.

KHAO NIAW
# STICKY RICE

400 g (2 cups) sticky rice

SERVES 4

PUT the rice in a bowl and pour in cold water to come 5 cm (2 inches) above the rice. Soak for at least 3 hours, or overnight. Drain and transfer to a bamboo basket specially made for steaming sticky rice, or to a steamer lined with a double thickness of muslin. Spread the rice in the steamer. Bring the water in the bottom of the steamer to a rolling boil. Taking care, set the rice over the water. Lower the heat, cover and steam for 20 to 25 minutes or until the rice swells and is glistening and tender. The cooking time will vary depending on the soaking time. Check and replenish the water every 10 minutes or so.

WHEN the rice is cooked, tip it onto a large tray and spread it out to help it cool quickly. If it cools slowly it will be soggy rather than sticky. Serve warm or cold.

KHAO NIAW KA-THI
# STEAMED STICKY RICE WITH COCONUT MILK

200 g (1 cup) sticky rice
170 ml (⅔ cup) coconut milk
  (page 279), well stirred
1 tablespoon palm sugar
  (not too brown)
½ teaspoon salt

SERVES 4

COOK the sticky rice according to the instructions in the recipe above.

WHILE the rice is cooking, stir the coconut milk, sugar and salt in a small saucepan over low heat until the sugar has dissolved. As soon as the rice is cooked, use a wooden spoon to gently mix it with the coconut milk. Set aside for 15 minutes.

NAAM PHRIK PHAO
## ROAST CHILLI SAUCE

80 ml (⅓ cup) oil
2 Asian shallots, finely chopped
2 garlic cloves, finely chopped
40 g (1½ oz) dried chilli flakes
¼ teaspoon palm sugar

MAKES 185 G (¾ CUP)

HEAT the oil in a small saucepan and fry the shallots and garlic until brown. Add the chilli flakes and palm sugar and stir well. Season with a pinch of salt. Use as a dipping sauce or accompaniment. The sauce can be stored in a jar in the refrigerator for several weeks.

NAAM JAEW
## CHILLI JAM

oil, for frying
20 Asian shallots, sliced
10 garlic cloves, sliced
3 tablespoons dried shrimp
7 dried long red chillies, chopped
3 tablespoons tamarind purée or
   3 tablespoons lime juice
6 tablespoons palm sugar
1 teaspoon shrimp paste

MAKES 250 G (1 CUP)

HEAT the oil in a wok or saucepan. Fry the shallots and garlic together until golden, then transfer from the wok to a blender or food processor.

FRY the dried shrimp and chillies for 1 to 2 minutes, then add these to the blender along with the remaining ingredients. Add as much of the frying oil as necessary to make a paste that you can pour. Put the paste back in the clean saucepan and bring to a boil. Reduce the heat and simmer until thick. Be careful because if you overcook this you will end up with a caramelized lump. Season the sauce with salt or fish sauce. Chilli jam is used as base for recipes, especially stir-fries, as well as a seasoning or accompaniment. It will keep for several months in an airtight jar in the refrigerator.

CHILLI JAM

NAAM JIM AAHAAN THALEH
## GARLIC AND CHILLI SAUCE

4 garlic cloves, finely chopped
3 bird's eye chillies, mixed red and
   green, stems removed, lightly
   crushed
2 tablespoons lime juice
1 tablespoon fish sauce
1 teaspoon sugar

MAKES 125 ML (½ CUP)

MIX all the ingredients together in a small bowl. The sauce can be stored in a jar in the refrigerator for several weeks.

GARLIC AND CHILLI SAUCE

PLUM SAUCE

PEANUT SAUCE

# SWEET CHILLI SAUCE

7 long red chillies, seeded and
   roughly chopped
185 ml (¾ cup) white vinegar
8 tablespoons sugar
½ teaspoon salt

MAKES 60 ML (¼ CUP)

USING a pestle and mortar or a small blender,
pound or blend the chillies into a rough paste.

IN a small saucepan, boil the vinegar, sugar and
salt over a high heat to boiling point, stirring
constantly. Reduce the heat to medium and
simmer for 15 to 20 minutes until the mixture
forms a thick syrup. Spoon the paste into the
syrup, cook for 1 to 2 minutes, then pour into
a bowl ready to serve.

NAAM JIM PLUM
# PLUM SAUCE

185 ml (¾ cup) white vinegar
8 tablespoons sugar
1 preserved plum (available in jars)
   without liquid

MAKES 60 ML (¼ CUP)

IN a small saucepan, heat the vinegar and sugar
quickly, stirring constantly, until it reaches boiling
point. Lower the heat to medium and simmer for
15 to 20 minutes until it forms a thick syrup.

ADD the preserved plum and mash it with a spoon
or fork. Cook for 1 to 2 minutes to form a smooth
paste, then pour into a bowl ready to serve.

NAAM SA-TE
# PEANUT SAUCE

2 garlic cloves, crushed
4 Asian shallots, finely chopped
1 lemon grass stalk, white part only,
   finely chopped
2 teaspoons Thai curry powder
   (page 287) or bought powder
1 tablespoon tamarind purée
1 tablespoon chilli paste
160 g (1 cup) unsalted roasted
   peanuts, roughly chopped
375 ml (1½ cups) coconut milk
   (page 279)
2 teaspoons palm sugar

MAKES 375 G (1½ CUPS)

HEAT 1 tablespoon vegetable oil in a saucepan
and fry the garlic, Asian shallots and lemon grass
for a minute. Add the Thai curry powder and stir
until fragrant.

ADD the remaining ingredients and bring slowly
to the boil. Add enough boiling water to make
a spoonable sauce and simmer for 2 minutes.
Season with salt to taste.

## KHAI KEM
# SALTED EGGS

10 fresh duck eggs (if available),
  or large chicken eggs, cleaned
175 g (6 oz) salt
a preserving jar, big enough to
  hold all the eggs

MAKES 10

IN a saucepan, heat 625 ml (2½ cups) water and the salt until the salt has dissolved. Allow to cool.

BEING very careful not to crack the shells, place the eggs into a large jar. Pour in the cool salt water. Seal the jar and leave for only three weeks. If you leave them any longer they will get too salty. Salted eggs will last for up to two months in their jar. Drain and use as required: boil the eggs, then scoop out the yolks and discard the whites.

## PHONG KARII
# CURRY POWDER

1 tablespoon black peppercorns
2 teaspoons white peppercorns
1 tablespoon cloves
3 tablespoons coriander seeds
3 tablespoons cumin seeds
1 tablespoon fennel seeds
seeds from 8 cardamom pods
3 tablespoons dried chilli flakes
2 tablespoons ground ginger
3 tablespoons ground turmeric

MAKES 125 G (½ CUP)

DRY-ROAST the peppercorns, cloves, coriander, cumin and fennel seeds, doing one ingredient at a time, in a frying pan over a low heat until fragrant.

TRANSFER to a spice grinder or pestle and mortar and grind to a powder. Add the remaining ingredients and grind together. Store in an airtight container.

CURRY POWDER

## AJAT
# CUCUMBER RELISH

4 tablespoons rice vinegar
125 g (½ cup) sugar
1 small red chilli, seeded and
  chopped
1 teaspoon fish sauce
80 g (½ cup) peanuts, lightly roasted
  and roughly chopped
1 Lebanese cucumber, unpeeled,
  seeded, finely diced

MAKES 185 G (¾ CUP)

PUT the vinegar and sugar in a small saucepan with 125 ml (½ cup) of water. Bring to the boil, then reduce the heat and simmer for 5 minutes.

ALLOW to cool before stirring in the chilli, fish sauce, peanuts and cucumber.

CUCUMBER RELISH

SALTED EGGS

# GLOSSARY OF THAI FOOD AND COOKING

**Asian shallots** *(hawn)* Small reddish-purple shallots used in South-East Asia. French shallots can be used instead.

**bamboo shoots** *(naw mai)* The edible shoots of bamboo. Available fresh when in season, otherwise preserved in jars or canned. Fresh shoots should be blanched (possibly more than once) if they are bitter.

**banana flower** *(hua plii)* **or blossom** This is the purple, teardrop-shaped flower of the banana plant. The purple leaves and pale yellow buds that grow between them are discarded. Only the inner pale core is eaten and this needs to be blanched in boiling water to remove any bitterness. It is advisable to wear rubber gloves to prepare banana flower as it has a gummy substance that can stain your fingers. Shredded banana flowers appear in salads and sometimes in curries.

**banana leaves** *(bai tawng)* Large green leaves, which can be used as a wrapping (dip briefly in boiling water or put in a hot oven for 10 seconds to soften them before use) for foods, or to line plates. Young leaves are preferable. Available from Asian food shops.

**bananas** *(kluay)* There are more than 20 different types of banana available in Thailand, all of which are used in cooking and are very popular. Varieties differ in flavour, with the small sugar bananas being the sweetest.

**basil** There are three types of basil used in Thai cuisine.

*Thai sweet basil (bai horapha)* is the most common. This has purplish stems, green leaves and an aniseed aroma and flavour. It is aromatic and is used in curries, soups and stir-fries, as well as sometimes being served as an accompaniment to *naam phrik*.

*Holy basil (bai ka-phrao)* is either red or green with slightly pointed, variegated leaves. Holy basil is used in stir-fries and fish dishes.

*Lemon basil (bai maeng-lak)* is also called mint basil. It is less common and is used in curries and stir-fries and as a condiment with rice noodles.

**bean curd** *see* tofu.

**betel leaves** *(bai cha-phluu)* Known also as piper leaves or wild tea leaves, these are not true betel but are a close relative. They are used to wrap some snacks. Use baby spinach leaves if you can't get betel leaves.

**black fungus** A funghi that is available fresh and dried, this has a cartilaginous texture and very little flavour. Dried fungus is soaked before use. It is used in Chinese-style soups and stir-fries.

**cardamom** *(luuk kra-waan)* A round white variety of cardamom is used in Indian- or Muslim-influenced curries such as massaman. Common green cardamom can be used instead.

Ready-ground cardamom quickly loses flavour. Use the pods whole or crushed.

**cha om** A bitter green vegetable resembling a fern. *Cha om* is used in omelette-style dishes and in stir-fries.

**chilli jam** *(naam jim phrik)* A thick, sweet chilli relish that can also be used as a sauce. Make it yourself (see page 283) or buy it ready-made.

**chilli sauce** The common name for siracha chilli sauce *(naam phrik sii raachaa)*, this is used more than any of the many other types of chilli sauce. Usually served alongside grilled fish, this thick orange sauce is named after the seaside town famous for its production. Chilli sauce goes with anything.

**chillies** *(phrik)* Red and green chillies are widely used in Thai cuisine. Recipes usually give a variety, rather than a colour. Generally, with Thai chillies, the smaller they are the hotter they are.

Bird's eye or mouse dropping chillies *(phrik khii nuu)* are the smallest and hottest. Most commonly green, but red can be used in most recipes.

Dragon's eye chillies *(phrik khii nuu suan)* are slightly larger and less hot.

Sky-pointing or long chillies *(phrik chii faa)* are about 5 cm (2 inches) in length and milder than the smaller ones. Used in stir-fries, salads and curry pastes.

Orange chillies *(phrik leuang)* are hot but not as hot as bird's eye chillies.

Banana chillies (phrik yuak) are large fat yellow/green (almost fluorescent) chillies with a mild flavour. They are used in stir-fries as well as in salads.

Dried chillies (phrik haeng) Dried red chillies are either long chillies or bird's eye. They are sometimes soaked in hot water to soften them. Remove the seeds if you prefer less heat.

Chinese kale (phak kaa-naa) Known as gai laan in Chinese food shops.

Chinese keys (kra-chai) A rhizome with skinny fingers that hang down like a bunch of keys. Has a peppery flavour. Available tinned, or preserved in jars, from Asian food shops.

cloves (kahn pluu) The dried, unopened flower buds of the clove tree. Brown and nail-shaped, they have a pungent flavour and so should be used in moderation. Use cloves whole or ground.

coconut (maphrao) The fruit of a coconut palm. The inner nut is encased in a husk which has to be removed. The hard shell can then be drained of juice before being cracked open to extract the white meat. Coconut meat is jellyish in younger nuts and harder in older ones. Medium-hard coconuts, which are perfect for desserts, are sold as grating coconuts in Thailand. The method for cracking and grating coconuts is shown on page 279.

coconut cream (hua ka-thi) This is made by soaking freshly grated coconut in boiling water and then squeezing out a thick, sweet coconut-flavoured liquid. It is available tinned but if you want to make your own, see page 279. Coconut cream is sometimes 'cracked' in order to fry curry pastes. This means it is boiled until the water evaporates out and it separates into oil and solids.

coconut milk (haang ka-thi) A thinner version of coconut cream, made as above but with more water or from a second pressing. Available tinned, but to make your own, see page 279.

coconut sugar (naamtaan maphrao) This sugar is made from the sap from coconut trees. Dark brown in colour, it is mainly used in sweet dishes. Palm sugar or unrefined soft brown sugar can be used instead.

coriander (phak chii) Fresh coriander leaves are used both as an ingredient and as a colourful garnish. The roots (raak phak chii) are chopped or ground and used in curry pastes and sauces. Buy bunches that have healthy green leaves and avoid any that are yellowing.

coriander seeds (met phak chii) The round seeds of the coriander plant have a spicy aroma and are used in some curry pastes, especially those that are Indian in style. To intensify the flavour, dry-roast the seeds until aromatic, before crushing them. Best freshly ground for each dish. They are available whole or ground.

corn (khao phoht) Now commonly grown in northern Thailand, corn is eaten freshly grilled as a healthy snack. Baby corn (khao phoht awn) is often used in stir-fries and curries.

cumin seeds (met yiiraa) The elongated ridged seeds of a plant of the parsley family, these have a peppery, slightly bitter flavour and are used in some curry pastes. To intensify the flavour, dry-roast the seeds before crushing them. Best freshly ground for each dish. Available whole or ground.

curry pastes (khreuang kaeng) Most often homemade in Thailand, though they can be bought freshly made in markets, and packaged in supermarkets. All curry pastes are ground and pounded together in a pestle and mortar until they are very smooth. The most common ones are red or hot (kaeng phet), green (kaeng khiaw-waan), panaeng or dry (kaeng phanaeng), matsaman or massaman (kaeng matsaman), sour orange (kaeng som), yellow (kaeng leuang), Chiang Mai or hangleh (kaeng hangleh) and jungle or forest (kaeng paa).

curry powder (phong karii) Usually bought ready-made in Thailand as it is not widely used except in a few stir-fries, marinades, sauces and in curry puffs.

dried fish (plaa haeng) Used extensively in Thai cuisine and a common roadside sight near the coast, dried fish is usually fried and crumbled and used in dips, salads and pastes.

dried shrimp (kung haeng) These are either ground until they form a fine fluff or rehydrated and used whole. Look for dark pink ones.

durian (thurian) The most infamous of fruit with a notoriously noxious aroma and sweet, creamy flavour and texture. It is banned from airlines and hotels.

eggplant (makheua) There are lots of varieties of eggplant (aubergine) used in Thai cuisine and, unlike in the West, bitterness is a prized quality. Common eggplants include Thai eggplant (ma-kheua phraw) which are pale green, orange, purple, yellow or white and golf-ball sized. Long eggplant (ma-kheua yao) are long, skinny and green. Pea eggplant (ma-kheau phuang) are tiny, bitter and look like large peas. Cut eggplant using a stainless steel knife and store in salted water to prevent them from turning black.

fish sauce (naam plaa) Made from salted anchovy-like fish that are left to break down naturally in the heat, fish sauce is literally the liquid that is drained off. It is the main source of salt flavouring in Thai cooking and is also used as a condiment. It varies in quality. Look for Tiparos or Golden Boy brands. A fermented version (naam plaa raa) is used in the North and North-East.

galangal or galingale *(khaa)* A rhizome, similar to ginger, used extensively in Thai cooking, usually in place of ginger. It is most famously used in *tom khaa kai*.

garlic *(kra-tiam)* Thai garlic has tiny cloves and is usually smashed with the side of a cleaver rather than being crushed before use. Deep-fried garlic is used as a garnish as is garlic oil. Deep-fried garlic can be bought in jars.

ginger *(khing)* The rhizome of a tropical plant which is sold in 'hands'. Fresh young ginger should have a smooth, pinkish beige skin and be firm and juicy. As it ages, the skin toughens and the flesh becomes more fibrous. Avoid old ginger which is wrinkled as it will be tough. Ginger is often measured in centimetre (inch) pieces and this means pieces with an average-sized width.

jackfruit *(kha-nun)* A large spiky fruit with segmented flesh enclosing large stones. It tastes like fruit salad and is used unripe in curries.

ketchap manis A thick, sweet soy sauce used as a flavouring.

lemon grass *(ta-khrai)* This ingredient is used in many Thai dishes. The fibrous stalk of a citrus perfumed grass, it is finely chopped or sliced or cut into chunks. Discard the outer layers until you reach a softer purple layer.

limes *(ma-nao)* Limes and lime juice are used extensively in Thai cuisine. Lime juice is a souring agent though Thai limes are sweeter than their Western counterparts. Lemon juice is not a particularly good substitute but can be used. Limes are often cut into cheeks rather than wedges.

lychees *(linchii)* Small round fruit with a red leathery skin and translucent white flesh surrounding a brown stone. Very perfumed and often available peeled and seeded in a syrup as a dessert.

makrut (kaffir) limes *(luk makrut)* These knobbly skinned fruit are used for their zest rather than their bitter juice. Leaves *(bai makrut)* are double leaves with a fragrant citrus oil. They are used very finely shredded or torn into large pieces. Frozen leaves are available but less fragrant than fresh ones.

mangoes *(ma-muang)* Green unripe mangoes are used in relishes, curries, soups and salads, or preserved in brine. Ripe mangoes are eaten out of the hand or alongside sticky rice as a dessert.

mint *(sa-ra-nae)* Mint is used in salads such as *laap* as well as being served alongside salads and rice-noodle soups.

mung bean sprouts *(thua ngawk)* These are used in stir-fries, soups and salads. Keep them in a bowl of cold water in the fridge to prolong their life.

mung beans *(thua leuang)* Whole beans are puréed or ground and used in desserts. Also used to make a type of noodle.

mushrooms *(het)* Straw mushrooms *(het faang)* are usually found tinned except in Asia. Replace them with oyster mushrooms if you need to. Shiitake *(het hawm)* are used both fresh and dried. Dried ones need to be soaked in boiling water before they are used.

noodles Rice noodles *(kuaytiaw)* are made of rice flour and water and steamed in sheets before being cut into widths. Wide line or *sen yai* noodles are about 2.5 cm (1 inch) wide, small line *(sen lek)* are 5 mm (¼ inch) in width and line noodles *(sen mii)* are 1–2 mm. Rice noodles are sold fresh and dried. The widths can be used interchangeably. Wheat noodles *(ba-mii)* are usually made with egg. Mung bean starch noodles *(wun sen)* are very thin white translucent noodles that go clear when soaked. They are much tougher than rice noodles. Both *wun sen* and *sen mii* are referred to as vermicelli.

oyster sauce Use the Thai version of the Chinese sauce if you can. It has a stronger oyster flavour.

palm sugar *(naamtaan piip)* Palm sugar is made by boiling sugar palm sap until it turns into a granular paste. Sold in hard cakes of varying sizes or as a slightly softer version in tubs. Malaysian and Indonesian brands of palm sugar are darker in colour and stronger in flavour. Unrefined, soft light brown sugar can be used instead.

pandanus leaves *(bai toey)* These long green leaves are shaped like blades and are used as a flavouring in desserts and sweets, as well as a wrapping for small parcels of food. Pandanus are also called screwpine. Essence can be bought in small bottles from speciality Asian food shops. Pandanus leaves are often sold frozen.

peanuts *(thua lisong)* Peanuts are used raw in some curries, deep-fried as a garnish, or in dipping sauces. Buy raw peanuts and fry them yourself for the best results.

peppercorns *(phrik thai)* Green peppercorns are used fresh in curries. Dried white peppercorns are used as a seasoning in dishes and as a garnish but black pepper is seldom used.

pickled garlic *(kra-tiam dong)* Eaten as an accompaniment, pickled garlic has a sweet/sour flavour. Preserved as whole heads that can be used as they are. Available at Chinese food shops.

pickled ginger *(khing dong)* Eaten as an accompaniment to curries and snacks. Buy ready-made from Asian food shops.

preserved cabbage *(phak gaund dong)* Salted and preserved cabbage is usually sold shredded. It sometimes comes in eathenware pots and is labelled Tianjin preserved vegetables. Available at Asian food shops.

**preserved plums** Salty, sour, preserved plums are used in sweet/sour dishes, to make plum sauce, and with steamed fish. Can be bought at Asian food shops.

**preserved radish** *(tang chai)* Salted and preserved radish is sold shredded or as strips. It is also referred to by the Japanese name, daikon, or the Indian, mooli. Comes salty and sweet/salty. Buy from Asian food shops.

**rambutan** *(ngaw)* A small round fruit with a red skin covered in soft, fine red spikes. Buy rambutan when they are vibrant in colour.

**rice** *(khao)* Jasmine (long-grain) and sticky rice are the two main varieties eaten in Thailand. Sticky rice comes in white and black, which is quite purple in reality. Much of the rice that is eaten is grown locally and it is nearly always white and polished. Jasmine rice is steamed, boiled or, more traditionally, cooked in a clay pot. Sticky rice is soaked and then steamed, either in a steamer or packed into lengths of bamboo.

**rice flour** *(paeng khao)* Made from white and black rice, this is also known as ground rice and is used in desserts.

**roasted chilli powder** *(phrik bon)* Both bird's eye and sky-pointing chilies are used to make chilli powder. Buy from Asian food shops or make your own by roasting and grinding whole chillies.

**roasted chilli sauce** *(naam phrik phao)* This sauce is made from dried red chillies roasted in oil, hence the name. It usually includes shrimp paste and palm sugar. Roasted chilli sauce comes in mild, medium and hot and is sold in jars and plastic pouches. To make your own, see page 283. Use as a flavouring and as a relish.

**rose apple** *(chom-phuu)* A crisp, watery fruit with no overwhelming taste, except for sweetness. Eaten on its own as a fruit and sometimes as an accompaniment to dips such as *naam phrik*.

**sago** *(saku)* Small dried balls of sago palm sap, which are used for milky desserts and savoury dishes. Cooked sago is transparent and soft with a silky texture.

**shrimp paste** *(ka-pi)* A strong smelling dark brownish-pink paste sold in small tubs that are usually sealed with wax. It is made from salted, fermented and dried shrimp. Buy a Thai version as those from other Asian countries vary. Used as it is or roasted first and refrigerated. This is very strong smelling and is a main ingredient in dips such as *naam phrik*.

**snake beans** *(thua fak yao)* Also called long beans or yard-long beans, these are sold in coils or tied together in bunches. Eaten fresh and cooked. Green beans can be used instead.

**sour sausage** Thai sausages can be bought ready-made or you can make them yourself (see page 42). They sometimes come wrapped in cellophane or banana leaves, or are strung together. Chinese sausages can be used instead.

**soy sauce** *(sii-yu)* Both light soy sauce *(sii-yu khao)* and dark soy *(sii-yu dam)* are used in Thai cooking. The dark one is sweeter than Chinese-style soy sauce.

**spring roll sheets** Wheat and egg dough wrappers that can be bought from Asian food shops and some good supermarkets. Look in the refrigerator or freezer sections. Squares of filo can also be used.

**tamarind** *(ma-khaam)* A fruit whose flesh is used as a souring agent. Usually bought as a dried cake or prepared as a purée, tamarind is actually a pod filled with seeds and a fibrous flesh. If you buy tamarind cake, then it must be soaked in hot water and then rubbed and squeezed to dissolve the pulp around the fibres. The fibres are then sieved out. Pulp is sold as purée or concentrate but is sometimes referred to as tamarind water in recipes. Freshly made tamarind water has a fresher, stronger flavour.

**tapioca flour** Made from ground, dried cassava root, this flour is used in desserts, dumpling wrappers and as a thickener. It is sold in small plastic bags in Asian food shops.

**tofu** *(tao-huu)* Also called bean curd, this can be firm or silken (soft).

**turmeric** *(kha-min)* A rhizome like ginger and galangal. In Thailand turmeric comes in white and yellow varieties. The yellow type is often referred to as red and is used fresh in curry pastes. Dried, it adds a yellow colour to curries, particularly Northern *khao sawy*. The white type is often eaten raw as a vegetable accompaniment to *naam phrik*.

**vinegar** *(naam som)* White coconut vinegar is the most common. Any mild white vinegar or better still, rice vinegar, can be used as a substitute.

**water spinach** *(phak bung)* Also called kang kong, morning glory, ong choy and water convolvulus, this is a leafy green vegetable that has hollow stems. Used as an ingredient as well as an accompaniment.

**wing beans** *(thua phuu)* Also called angle beans, these have four frilly edges. Used cut into cross sections in salads and stir-fries. Buy as fresh as you can.

**won ton sheets** These sheets or wrappers are available from the refrigerator or freezer cabinets of Asian food shops. Some are yellow and include egg in the pastry and others are white. Gow gee and gyoza wrappers can also be used.

**yellow bean sauce** *(tao jiaw)* This paste made of yellow soy beans adds a salty flavour to dishes.

# INDEX

# BIBLIOGRAPHY

Bhumichitr, Vatcharin, *The Taste of Thailand*, Pavilion Books, 1988.

Cummings, Joe, *World Food Thailand*, Lonely Planet, 2000.

Davidson, Alan, *Oxford Companion to Food*, Oxford University Press, 1999.

Hargreave, Oliver, *Exploring Chiang Mai, City, Valley and Mountains*, Within Books, 1997.

Loha-Unchit, Kasma, *It Rains Fishes, Legends, Traditions and the Joys of Thai Cooking*, Pomegranate Art Books, 1995.

Solomon, Charmaine, *Encyclopedia of Asian Food*, Hamlyn, 1996.

Thompson, David, *Classic Thai Cuisine*, Ten Speed Press, 1993.

Thompson, David, *Thai Food*, Chrysalis Books, 2002.

Yu, Su-Mei, *Cracking the Coconut, Classic Thai Home Cooking*, William Morrow, 2000.

# THE FOOD OF THAILAND

This edition first published in Canada in 2005 by Whitecap Books,
351 Lynn Ave., North Vancouver, British Columbia, Canada, V7J 2C4.

www.whitecap.ca

ISBN 1 55285 682 8
ISBN 978 1 55285 682 6

First published in 2003 by Murdoch Books Pty Limited.
© Text, design, photography and illustrations Murdoch Books Pty Limited

Food Editor: Lulu Grimes
Recipes: Oi Cheepchaiissara   www.modernthaifood.com
Additional Recipes: Ross Dobson
Design Concept: Marylouise Brammer
Designer: Susanne Geppert
Production: Fiona Byrne
Editorial Director: Diana Hill
Editor: Wendy Stephen
Photographer (location and recipes): Alan Benson
Additional Photography (recipes): Ian Hofstetter
Stylist: Mary Harris
Additional Styling: Katy Holder
Stylist's Assistant: Wendy Quisumbing
Map: Berit Kruger-Johnsen

Publisher: Kay Scarlett
Chief Executive: Juliet Rogers

PRINTED IN CHINA by C & C Offset Printing Co. Ltd. in 2005. Reprinted 2006.

## ACKNOWLEDGMENTS

The Publisher wishes to thank the following for all their help in making this book possible:

The Dusit Group: Werachej Lelanuja, Jakkris Supeerajit, Holger Jakobs, Andrew Swatdipakdi, Saravuth Manuthasna,
Victor Sukseree, Chanok Chaisiri, Ingo Räuber, Peter Held; Randall Marketing: Angela Blair; World Travel Services:
Jack Painchokdee, Praphan Jandeng; Thailand Tourist Board Australia: Leanne Ward; Valcom: Ms. Huai Hui Lee,
Ms. Chritravee Suwanag, Mr. Vitsnu Pongsmai; Tang Sang Hah Co. Ltd.: Worachet Pongpairoj, Jarin Pongpairoj,
Patiphan Pongpairoj, Kobkiat Pongpairoj, Marosak, V. (QC), Ekaphol Chueroongrueng; Chiang Mai Thai Cookery School:
Sompon and Elizabeth Nabnian, Pom and all the staff; Chia Meng Co. Ltd.: Mr. Tavol Manathanya, Mrs. Prapit Manathanya,
Mrs. Mayura Manathanya, Mr. Somsak Kamjornkitbaworn, Ms. Walaiporn Phuhiran; Mei Kim Lui factory, Phetchaburi;
Oriental Merchant: Hannah Yiu.